"In the grand tradition

of the courageous curmudgeon, H. L. Mencken, and the legendary Beat poet Anne Waldman, James Botsford's new book, *Rants and Riffs*, gives a shout-out to not only the myriad hypocrisies of the day, but sings mellifluous hymns of praise to friendship, love, and nature. Here are eviscerating essays on politics, ritual rants, humorous teases, literary philippics, and textured riffs on the absolute necessity of fighting for justice. This book goes a long way to proving the truth of Hemingway's call for writers to make damned sure that they use a *'built-in, shockproof, bullshit detector'* in their search for that elusive creature called truth."

Phil Cousineau, author of *Once and Future Myths, The Book of Roads,* and *The Hero's Journey: The Life and Work of Joseph Campbell*

Rants
Riffs

. . .

ESSAYS WITH ATTITUDES

by

James Botsford

Sandyhouse Press

ISBN: 9780983311058
Library of Congress Control Number: 2017916340

Copyright © 2018 James Botsford

Sandyhouse Press
9004 Hollirob Lane
Wausau, Wisconsin 54403
www.thebigsandy@gmail.com

Book design and cover photo by
Steve Stolee, *Stolee Communications*

Printed on Glatfelter paper in Wausau, Wisconsin

Other books by James Botsford

You Should Write that Down

Them Apples

The Wisconsin Tribal Judges Association:
A Documentary History

For Krista

who finds in the wind
what it takes me decades to write.

Acknowledgments

Thanks to my early critical readers: Jim McKenzie, Phil Sorensen, and David Keefe. To Phil Cousineau, trusty font of key seasoned ideas. To Mary Jo Nyenhuis for preparing the pages. To Jackie O'Brien and Krista Botsford for some last looks corrections. Thanks to Steve Stolee for expert design, layout, and badinage. And a deep bow to Phil Sorensen for the best keen-eyed editing a guy like me ever had.

A version of "The Big Conversation" first appeared in *Toward a Whole Which is Greater, Why the Wisconsin Uprising Failed,* published by *Wipf and Stock,* 2012, used with permission of the editors. A version of "Postcard From the New Delhi Night" first appeared in *Burning the Midnight Oil,* by Phil Cousineau, published by Viva Editions, 2013, used with permission of the author. Various versions of "So They Sued Us" have appeared on the websites www.enbridgesuedus.com and www.GoFundMe.com.

Contents

Rants

Riffs

. . .

PREFACE

Rant: A high-flown, extravagant, or bombastic speech or utterance; a piece of turgid declamation; a tirade.

Examples of early usage found in the Oxford English Dictionary:

1641: *The more the merrier, I'm resolved to rant it to the last.*

1647: *They say you're angry, and rant mightily.*

1668: *I left my client yonder in a rant against the envious, and the ignorant.*

1717: *What I looked upon as a rant... I now begin to think a serious truth.*

1725: *How heartsome... to hear the birds chirm o'er their pleasing rants.*

1735: *I have heard some of your priests ranting highly against our translation.*

1781: *In such a cause I grant an English poet's privilege to rant.*

Riff: A melodic phrasing, often repeated, accompanying a singular theme. Traced to musicians a hundred years ago.

Jimi Hendrix's Voodoo Child voted best guitar riff.

A monologue or spoken improvisation, especially a humorous one, on a particular subject.

You get the idea.

Bottom of the Totem Pole

L adies and Gentlemen, I am convinced of the innate principle of human nature that almost everyone wants someone lower than themselves on the totem pole of life. And here in America we put Indians there. Always lower than Blacks, Chicanos, other ethnicities. So low they don't even show up on the ethnic category lists on most Gallup polls, government reports or any other demographics likely to be compiled. We like to measure ethnicities. Take their pulse, see how they're doing. But when it comes to Indians we have covered over so much awfulness, we find it best not to look under the rug.

Even the popes in days of old declared it okay to kill indigenous people. A series of Papal Bulls in the 15th Century created the "Doctrine of Discovery" and justified, in believers' minds, the raw theft and carnage perpetrated under religious auspices. This history can be traced through the book *Pagans in the Promised Land: Decoding the Doctrine of Christian Discovery* by Steven Newcomb, 2008, Fulcrum Publishing.

The reasoning described in those Papal Bulls is that since indigenous people were not Christian and did not have souls they were not fully human, so take everything – even their lives. No blame, no shame, no crime, no guilt, no shit. Clean and tidy Papal bull.

And so we did. Their land and hair and children. Even robbed their graves – put 'em in a dead museum. A white one. The horrors and shame and thievery too staggeringly big to face, so we keep them on the bottom of the totem pole and only report their failings and mistakes. We stole the totem pole from them, as well. But we perverted the meaning. Indigenous cultures from the Himalayas to the Pacific Northwest conceptualize in their totems the symbiotic interrelationships of all life. Finding such sensibilities too messy and archaic, the Christians turned the totem pole into a hierarchy of self-serving values. Hence, the low-man.

Only Indians could we shoot and loot indiscriminately without penalty or shame. Even the slaves had their papers, their rights to the chains of slavery. But, Jesus Christ, what would Jesus Christ say? The later Christians created this hierarchy, and still won't put Indians on the national chart.

Don't you dare think I'm ranting only about our ancestors long ago. I'm talking about former Chief Justice William Rehnquist and his most Christian brethren on our sacrosanct Supreme Court right now. They will take an Indian case, Rehnquist called them "shit cases" off the record (*The Brethren*, Woodward and Armstrong, 1993). The high Court will spend dozens of pages convoluting logic and dignity and history to reach their dismissive result; Indians have no protected rights to their cultures or their religions. Their ceremonies, their sacred sites cannot be considered sacred – no buildings, no texts. Their pagan ceremonies are not institutionalized enough to respect as valid. We use the same kind of reductionistic logic when it comes to tribal sovereignty. Since the courts cannot deny the treaties exist, they interpret them into oblivion one chink at a time unless it's just the right case, then they take a big chunk out of the sovereignty that remains. It takes a lot of ink, but hey, we have a lot of ink.

Everyone likes to have someone lower on the totem pole than themselves. Think about it, Ladies and Gentlemen. We idolize Einstein who said all things are relative and therefore related. But for how many centuries have Native people continued sitting in solemn circles of ceremony right here in the so-called land of the free chanting Mitakuye Oyasin – "All My Relations." Wisdom passed down and sung about. Knowledge that all things are related, all have life, all are interdependent, all are therefore sacred - rock and tree and you and me and the sun above and the deep blue sea. Yet here we sit, erstwhile bosses of destiny paying each other to soil our own nest while the cops and courts and Congress take yet another bite out of the dignified rights of tribes.

Oh, great magnanimity. We honor them as mascots of our favorite teams. Teams we love. Teams we appreciate. Teams that mean something to us. But do you think Indians are grateful? No, the Natives are restless. We can't make caricature mascots out of the Blacks, Chicanos, or Jews any more. Couldn't the Indians just let us have our fun? Don't they have worse problems to attend to? I heard the reservations are awful. Do they live in houses? Why don't they just move to town?

Oh, great melting pot on the altar of America. Let us, quietly if we can, absorb those Indian eyes. Let us, without articulated malice anymore, but with ink and ignorance and self-righteous pride insist that in the end, for their own good, they must melt in our pot.

You think these indignities are not happening? Of course you think they are not happening. You think it's broadcast on CNN or FOX or even PBS? Only when the Indians make whiteman-sized mistakes. Or maybe for an hour once in a while on the Nature channel.

Ladies and Gentlemen, is it human nature or damn near so that everyone wants someone lower than their own group on the totem pole of life? A sad and fraudulent hierarchy to make us feel better about ourselves. With all the terror, dishonor, and the pox of merciless deceit we have perpetrated against those who were here first, it serves us well to put them on the bottom and to keep them there. Where we know we got 'em. And not report on the facts, the truth, or their generosity of spirit which somehow quietly survives.

I'M NOT GOING TO LIE

There are a few words and phrases in contemporary English usage that make me cringe. One of them is the title of this rant. Many people these days, particularly but not exclusively young people, will throw that ridiculous phrase on the front end of an otherwise perfectly worthy statement. These are otherwise kind and intelligent people. Might be a close friend or relative, or maybe someone you've just met. It's an equally disastrous thing to say whether or not you know the speakers. If it was simply a superfluous phrase I could roll with it. But it's not. It's flat out embarrassing.

What does it mean when a rational person with whom you are speaking prefaces a statement with, "I'm not going to lie…"? Does it mean:

> *"Although I have a nasty propensity for being dishonest, in this instance I want you to know I am making a real effort to tell the truth."*

Or does it mean:

> *"I want you to know that while I could just as easily be deceitful in what I'm about to say you should feel good that I've suddenly decided to be honest with you."*

Or is it part of a twelve step treatment plan to overcome a chronic bad habit?

> *"Hello. My name's Bill and I'm not going to lie."*

If that's what it is, fine. But perhaps just say it silently to yourself.

Equally mindless and grating is the closely related phrase, "To be honest with you…" What the hell is the listener supposed to infer from that?

> *"Although our conversation on this topic may not warrant such respect, I have nonetheless chosen to be truthful and wanted to let you know that up front."*

These two phrases are worse than useless. Even if they are just inartful ways of trying to emphasize the next thought, they're embarrassing. If you want to emphasize what you are about to say, use a little inflection, or wiggle your goddamn eyebrows.

The word "awesome" stands as another abomination which has befallen our beloved English language. Although this travesty is now in perhaps its third decade, it still makes me want to weep. The world knows English is bereft of spiritual terminology. The Dalai Lama, who knows a thing or two about such matters, says English, although an uncommonly effective language for some purposes, simply does not have words for many aspects of spiritual considerations. You don't have to dig very deep into languages like Sanskrit, Tibetan, Chinese, or Hindi for examples to understand that point.

It was particularly deflating to watch the pathetic expropriation of the word awesome – one of the few sacred words in English reduced to emptiness by everyone from Valley Girls to congressmen. Now used to describe a new flavor of ice cream or the paint job on your cousin's pick up truck.

Yet another example of the decadent slippage of our vocabulary: when people died we used to say they were dead or that they died. You might hear someone say they had passed away, which has a hint of presumption about an afterlife. Occasionally you'd hear that someone passed on, which has a stronger inference of Valhalla or other heavenish place for your wonderful personality to be immortalized.

But more and more these days when someone dies, I'm being told they "passed." I'm not sure if this is some P.C. affectation or what, but I do know it is palpably laden with feigned amorphous presumptions which at best overstate hopes. And to make it worse, it's shorthand, an abbreviation, slangish.

"Did you hear about Joe? He passed." He passed what? Gas? Some people pass kidney stones – which scream out painfully. And, of course, I pass a lot of cars. But I know when the significant-to-me event of my death occurs, I want people to look each other in the eye and say I died. I don't want them equating me to a fart, or a kidney stone, or a Chevrolet.

And don't get me started on the abuse not only of language, but also of perception resulting from the mindless insertion of the word "like" into nearly every other descriptive or declarative sentence by hordes of young Americans. Is it like they can't seem to say anything without deferring to a simile? No it isn't. It is, in fact, they can't seem to say anything without cloaking it as a simile. But a simile it is not. A simile requires a comparison or a contrast. This lazy abuse of "like" compares a thing to itself and, as such, is a one-legged affair that doesn't go anywhere. Takes two to tango. Putting a perfectly good simile word in a one-legged single-pointed sentence is as useless as tits on a boar. Worse. Tits on a boar would bother neither man nor beast. In fact, I've come to believe it's even worse than that. Turning all of one's verbal expressions into pseudo-similes may have the effect of turning one's perceptions, one's experiences of life into similes. Perhaps it is a tell-tale symptom of spending too much time in virtual realities, altering our perceptions with simulated living. Regardless, it either sucks or it blows. Pick a direction. Either way, I don't care.

Ranting takes a lot of energy, so I picked up my friend Jim and we went down to the coffee shop to take a break. When the barista brought our coffee to the table, Jim said thanks, to which the barista replied, "No problem." Jim looked up at her and asked, "Why, was it almost a problem? Had you been expecting it to be a problem to bring our coffee and are so relieved it wasn't that you just had to share the good news?" She gave Jim a perplexed and displeased look, but we hoped she sorted out what he meant as she walked away. I like Jim. He's an old fart, but he rocks the rant.

In a moment that calls for something gracious, or at least polite, why would anyone choose a harsh quasi-negative phrase that implies they just went out of their way to do you a favor? Indeed, why would you say such a thing when the act for which you have been thanked is the job you are paid to do?

And it is equally grating in more personal exchanges. When I offer my granddaughter an ice cream cone and she looks at me with those beautiful wondrous eyes and says thanks, I sure hope I always find something more thoughtful to reply than, "No problem."

To be honest with you (I'm not going to lie) it's been awesome (like, no problem) getting this crap off my chest, because at any moment I could pass.

I Think I'm a Conservative, but the Republicans Tell Me No

"Should any political party attempt to abolish social security, unemployment insurance and eliminate labor laws and farm programs, you would not hear of that party again in our political history. There is a tiny splinter group, of course, that believes you can do these things. Among them are H.L. Hunt (you possibly know his background), and a few other Texas oil millionaires and an occasional politician or business man from other areas. Their number is negligible and they are stupid." – President Eisenhower in a letter to his brother Edgar in 1954

That is how things looked to a Republican leader in 1954. Let us look under the hood of today's political machinery.

It's fair to say generally speaking Democrats are ineffectual, fiscally less responsible, tend to coddle the disenfranchised, and are more eager to throw money and regulations at problems. And it's fair to say Republicans are more selfish, less compassionate, and more clever and bold in disingenuously manipulating language and law to achieve short-sighted goals.

But it isn't fair to call Democrats liberals, and even less fair these days to call Republicans conservative. For one thing, the confusion arising from letting such terms pass as synonyms creates false polarities that distract us from the work of reasoned governance. For another thing, in the Republicans case especially, it is a ruse. It's a misleading subterfuge behind which some very self-serving right wing ideology has continued to play out.

I think I'm more conservative than the Republicans – though you wouldn't know it from my voting record. It would sure be helpful if journalists at least would stop conflating the terms "Republican" and "Conservative". That would help shine a ray of light on a clever and confusing charade.

"Conservatives today would have us believe they are the voice of American values. In fact, they are not even the voice of

conservative values." – Mickey Edwards, former Chair of the House Republican Policy Committee, and former Chair of the American Conservative Union

Today's Republicans act more like an apocalyptic cult than a reasonable voice of civility. With their vitriolic and hypocritical claptrap they profess to revere the Constitution on one hand and caustically denigrate, even subvert, the government it creates. They fight tooth and nail for billionaire hedge fund managers to pay a lower income tax than teachers and firemen. They enact and support policies that allow giant U.S. based corporations to pay no income tax whatsoever on one hand and proclaim we cannot afford Medicare, unemployment insurance, and Social Security on the other.

Somebody stole the word *conservative*. Let us see what they have done:

Keeping the Government Out of My Personal Life.

This represents a classic bastion of conservative precepts. The government has no business caring whether I am straight or gay; no business in manipulating access to birth control; no business in requiring a trans-vaginal wand to be inserted into my wife or any other woman.

But the Republicans tell me No. They want to impose limitations and restrictions on non-heterosexuals that do not apply to others. They want to shut down Planned Parenthood offices. They want to overturn Roe v. Wade. They want to create a humiliating if not impossible path of access for women to get lawful abortions. Yet Barry Goldwater's wife was a founding Board Member of Planned Parenthood in Arizona. Today's Republicans try their best to discredit and defund Planned Parenthood. This may appeal to their so-called "base" of evangelicals and misogynists, but it's a million miles away from traditional conservative values.

Non Interventionist Foreign Policies

It used to be that conservatives would rail against getting into wars and other political quagmires in other parts of the world. They would caution against intervention in all but the most dire circumstances. I share that view. We should not be the world's policeman or moral arbiter. Partly because it's too expensive and messy, and partly because we don't know what we're doing and are a bunch of xenophobes who are ridiculously overconfident that we know what's right.

"If we justify war it is because all peoples always justify the traits of which they find themselves possessed."– Ruth Benedict

But the Republicans tell me No. They want us to throw our weight around. We're Number One! American Exceptionalism! The "Military industrial complex" of which President Eisenhower (Republican) warned us is now ubiquitous. It is revered and unchallenged, championing the defense spending that eats us alive. We are not even embarrassed or talking about it. Senators McCain and Graham, supposedly our "foreign policy experts" in the Senate, offer knee-jerk, belligerent military solutions to nearly every significant world crisis. And I still believe Bush and Cheney should be charged with war crimes in the international court for the invasion of Iraq.

"War, like any other racket, pays high dividends to the very few…. The cost of operations is always transferred to the people who do not profit." – General Smedley Butler

As of this writing we find ourselves further stymied with the abhorrent burden of Donald Trump as President. Time might prove me tragically wrong, but he arrives as a deviant aberration. Because of his individualized personality disorders, we need not consider him ideologically significant. Or so I hope.

Conservation of Resources

This one's got the word "conserve" built right into it. Should be a no-brainer a conservative would want to be careful to conserve things. Save for a rainy day. Not foul your own nest in an overly eager, zesty exploitation of resources. Don't assume the sky's the limit. And don't assume there's pie in the sky. We have a future to plan for, the world of our grandchildren; to say nothing of seven generations hence. We also have values to conserve and pass on, qualities of life.

But the Republicans tell me No. They want to repeal the Clean Air Act. Repeal the Clean Water Act. Dismantle the Environmental Protection Agency. Get government out of the way of "Progress." And that definition of progress is so clever, slippery, and amorphous that it has the power of a religious precept. Like one of the Ten Commandments, except you can do just about anything in its name.

I do not expect anyone would doubt the vast majority of climate change deniers are Republican. But are they conservative? In recent years powerful funders have spent hundreds of millions of dollars denying scientific findings about climate change. I don't think anyone would doubt the vast majority of these powerful funders are Republicans. But are they conservative? Conservatives used to be careful stewards of the environment.

"We live beyond our means by... insatiably devouring minerals and forests and the very soil, lowering the water table, to gratify the appetites of the present tenants of the country." – Russell Kirk, "The Conservative Mind," 1953

Public Education

"At the desk where I sit, I have learned one great truth. The answer for all our national problems – the answer for all the problems of the world – comes to a single word. That word is 'education.' – Lyndon B. Johnson

I grew up in a conservative household where I was taught the values of a good public education. Where every kid has an equal chance to learn and become whomever they want. It was a matter of civic pride to have good, well-rounded public schools for everyone. We understood the equal playing field for all the kids, to which every taxpayer contributed, as part of the real genius of America. We considered good public education the heart of good citizenship, a strong conservative value. I believe in a good and equal public education system, just like my conservative daddy did.

But the Republicans tell me No. They are eagerly and insidiously determined to dismantle this bastion of American life and have managed to do a lot in that direction already. Attacking teachers' unions and slashing budgets for education has caused the public schools to decline. All of which fits perfectly with a private enterprise based agenda of privatizing education through the proliferation of charter schools and voucher schools. It is hard to imagine a less conservative approach to the future of this country. It surely is the opposite of conservative, though I'm not sure what

to call it... maybe dangerous and flippant and unfounded.
"All who have meditated on the art of governing mankind have been convinced that the fate of empires depends on the education of youth." – Aristotle (384-322 B.C.)

America Must Guard Against Oligarchy

Here we arrive at the core of our democratic principles. Conservative thinking has long valued the equality inherent in democratic theory. None of that old European feudalism for us. I agree.

An oligarchy vests all its power in a few people, a dominant class, or a clique. Much of the world looks like this. But one of the virtues of American conservatism has been its historic insistence on democratic principles as a guard against all the other inbred and constricted systems. I think the liberals, progressives, and no-names would agree: resisting oligarchy has been a solid principle of conservative thinking. So even though I feel confident I share a fundamental conservative principle here... the Republicans tell me No. In fact, the Republicans do not seem troubled by the Citizens United decision, handed down by the "conservative" majority of the U.S. Supreme Court. The loss of America's foundational feature of egalitarianism is like water off the back of a modern Republican duck.

"We can have democracy in this country or we can have great wealth concentrated in the hands of a few, but we cannot have both." – Justice Louis D. Brandeis

America Must Guard Against Plutocracy

Here we are still at the core of our democratic principles. Plutocracy means government by the wealthy. Technically, it represents something different than oligarchy. Rather than control by family dynasties, it is a cult of the wealthy and powerful. In a pragmatic sense it is not much different than oligarchy, especially since Citizens United. The "party of Lincoln" used to stand for encouraging voter participation and then letting the majority rule, with the Bill of Rights safeguards always waiting in the wings. Makes sense to me.

But the Republicans tell me No. Contemporary Republican

strategists are complicit in a secret plan to consolidate power in the hands of the wealthy (read white) as a countermeasure to the inevitable demography that shows the "browning of America" or, as my Native teachers taught me, the *"re*-browning of America." Republican leadership proceeds shamelessly, with a straight face, trying their best to reduce the taxes on the wealthy and deregulate all the financial market shenanigans.

> *"Anybody has a right to evade taxes if he can get away with it. No citizen has a moral obligation to assist in maintaining government."* – *J.P. Morgan*

Private Property Rights Versus Corporate 'Rights'

My wife and I own some prime quality farm land in the Red River Valley of North Dakota. Our land has been in the family for decades, and when my parents died some of it came to us. We don't live there anymore so we rent it out to neighboring farm families, some of whom we have worked with for generations. When we inherited this land we told our children we intended to keep it, be good stewards, and pass it on to them when we die – meanwhile relying on the rental income to supplement our retirement.

So when Enbridge Pipeline Corporation asked permission to cross our land with a 24" pipeline that would pump up to 300,000 barrels of oil per day from the Bakken Oil Fields of western North Dakota to Superior, Wisconsin, then loaded on ships and sent wherever the market paid the most, we said no. We explained how we choose to protect the integrity of the property for posterity and did not want to risk ruining the land with a break in the line. We cited the hundreds of breaks and leaks in Enbridge lines in recent years, including one in Michigan that rivaled the Exxon Valdez Oil spill. We told Enbridge we invest in sustainable energy alternatives and want to do what we can to reduce the carbon in the atmosphere in order to conserve a healthy environment for the future. In other words, we took what might be considered a conservative position.

Enbridge Pipeline (which is based in Canada, but "registered" in North Dakota) told me I didn't seem to understand. They said they weren't really asking us, they were telling us they're coming through our land. They said the state of North Dakota had agreed to designate them a "public utility" and thereby gave them quasi-governmental powers of eminent domain to condemn our land for purposes of their 99-year easement...but they would give us some money in exchange. We told them we would not give them an easement across our land, so they sued us. Thus began a legal battle. The results are discussed elsewhere in this book under the title "So They Sued Us."

Well, we thought, at least this time our conservative friends and relatives will be on our side as individual property owners fighting against a giant outside corporation in cahoots with government trying to take our private property.

But the Republicans told me No. Our "conservative" friends and relatives stood on the other side. They expressed frustration, even embarrassment we would insist on what we considered good old fashioned conservative principles when it meant going against "progress" and "business."

Disposable Materialism

To be conservative implies, nay insists, by nature one tends to conserve things, to value what one has, make do as needed, and be repulsed by the careless extravagance of disposable materials.

But the Republicans tell me No. They insist pro-business is such an important consideration it leaves such conservation values in the ditch — alongside the plastic bottles and bags.

Work is Better than Welfare

Government policies which result in more people working and fewer on the dole are a good thing. But it does not simply happen, especially after a recession. Nor does relying on trickle down economic policies. In the years when trickle down policies have prevailed, the rich have gotten richer and unemployment has gone up. Like anything else if you want something to work well you have to invest some energy into it. Lots of people are out of work through no fault of their own. They get caught in the negatives of the recent recession (brought about by people who benefited from its causes and/or effects), and by Republican sponsored pro-corporate policies favoring outsourcing. When you add to those factors the people who never have worked, including those who are second or third generation on welfare, you're talking about millions of people unemployed. Common sense insists creating policies and programs putting those folks to work and teaching them skills is a smart investment. At the same time, as it happens, we have crumbling infrastructure in our country and other massive problems we claim we cannot afford to address. Well, FDR addressed similar conditions with the Works Project Administration and the Civilian Conservation Corps. The country got better physically and a lot of good citizens went to work, learned new marketable skills, provided for their families and took pride in contributing to their country. A plan a conservative could not only support, but insist on.

But the Republicans tell me No. It's a little hard to puzzle out their reasoning by applying, well, reason. But in the myopic gobbledygook they offer, you hear things like praise for the trickle down policies of yesteryear, knee-jerk rejection of anything that could be construed as a government program, and a blather of platitudes blaming the poor and the unemployed.

The Right to Vote

This is a bedrock principle of the bread and butter of democracy. Nothing more down to earth and conservative than the sacrosanct right to vote when it comes to preserving (conserving) the genius of our democratic system. Shouldn't be any disagreement here. Respecting the integrity of our system of government is a value long championed by conservatives. Use it or lose it, I used to hear. Everyone has a duty to exercise his or her right to vote. That's what makes our country great.

But the Republicans tell me No. They will throw such grand notions under the bus in order to win their agenda. The shenanigans in Florida in the 2000 presidential race were incredibly unprincipled. The Republican power structure obstructed the rights of thousands to vote in districts which leaned Democrat, and then the "conservatives" on the U.S. Supreme Court gave it a stamp of approval. But it only emboldened them. Now the Republican Party in a growing number of states is promoting, and successfully enacting, legislation making it harder for some people to vote (by "some people" I mean demographic groups that tend to vote Democrat). So-called Voter ID laws and other restrictive ploys are transparently manipulative of a citizen's basic and fundamental right to participate in our democracy. It strikes me as a national embarrassment at best, or worse, an indicator of the decline of civilization.

Professor Justin Levitt of the Loyola University School of Law, an expert in constitutional law and the law of democracy, with a particular focus on election administration and redistricting, has investigated every allegation of voter fraud made over the past 14 years. He found only 31 instances (not all actual prosecutions, but all reported instances) in which a person was accused of casting a ballot under someone else's name. That is a mere 31 instances in every election in the U.S. since 2000 – a period in which more than one billion votes were cast. Thirty-one instances of voter fraud in one billion votes – that is less than one illegitimate vote for every thirty-two million two hundred fifty-eight thousand votes cast! Levitt points out other kinds of voter fraud do occur, such as vote buying and ballot stuffing by corrupt officials, but Voter ID laws do nothing to prevent those things. He concludes Voter ID laws will do nothing to make elections cleaner, but they will prevent millions of legitimate voters from casting ballots.

"Bad officials are elected by good citizens who do not vote."
– George Jean Nathan

Family Farming

As I was growing up, I thought most farmers were conservative. Conservative thinking and farming as a livelihood go together like the chicken and the egg. It is a wholesome, independent, self-sufficient, private enterprise, with family values, meat and potatoes, an American vocation from the earliest years of the USA.

But the Republicans tell me No. Turns out family farming, while a noble profession to everyone, including liberals and conservatives, is increasingly contrary to the Republican agenda. The push to promote corporate farming is pretty much always led by the Republicans in every state. Better to call them "corporatists" than "conservatives." All the virtues associated with family owned and operated farms get pushed to the back burner when they run contrary to the interests of Cargill, Monsanto, General Foods, Kraft, Tyson, Nestle. It is breathtaking to watch Republicans jump on the corporate agribusiness bandwagon regardless of its devastating impact on family farming. Perhaps worse, that model does not seriously address the long-term health of the land and the quality of the food it produces.

The Egalitarian Virtues of the Estate Tax

Congress created the estate tax for dual purposes. There is the obvious purpose of raising money for the federal coffers. But behind that purpose was, and is, an important principled reason that appealed to conservatives and liberals. The estate tax supplies a vital way we Americans protect ourselves from drifting into an old European-style feudalism where property ownership increasingly belongs to fewer and fewer families through unchecked accumulation over generations.

The estate tax mitigates against the concentration of wealth by taxing a deceased's assets above a certain amount at a high rate. By requiring large estates to liquidate some assets to pay the tax, it puts those assets back in circulation for others to acquire. It is a modest but effective hedge against a drift toward feudalism. It helps protect family farmers by keeping giant farms from growing exponentially. Sounds like a good, conservative plan.

But the Republicans tell me No. As is their forte, they have used fear and hyperbole to turn a virtuous policy into something they call The Death Tax. Same law, new scary name. The estate tax only affects multi-millionaires, but the Republicans would have you believe it is unraveling the fabric of our families and farms.

And, by the way, speaking of the Republican ideologues' deceptive manipulation of language, the "entitlement" of social security they claim is a government program we can't afford is actually an "earned benefit" you and I already paid for.

Strangely enough, the Republicans' positions on government regulation have slowly drifted into such a mishmash of hypocritical inconsistencies that identifying a pattern requires a contortionist's flexibility. Disillusioned Republican party insiders and professional pundits have written books on the subject of inconsistent Republican policies, so let's just look at the larger trends of this phenomenon. These are dangerous trends, because the positions are simultaneously antithetical to foundational principles, yet espoused as truly "American."

Here are some examples: The get-government-off-my-back-and-out-of-my-personal-life Republicans want to interfere with a woman's right to reproductive choices to the point of (among other things) urging legislation requiring trans-vaginal wands be inserted into women's vaginas. Get government off my back and into my wife's uterus. Republicans also avidly promote regulations requiring ongoing blood or saliva screenings for any poor person receiving public benefits. And the Republicans not only authored most of the personally intrusive privacy invasion provisions of the Patriot Act, but continue to fight against the ACLU and others who champion resistance to the heavy-handed Big Brother nature of many of those unnecessarily intrusive provisions.

Conclusion

One hopes clarity emerges from the cloudy hodgepodge of misnomers and co-opted principles. Why is it so hard to see how the Grand Old Party got hijacked by self-serving power brokers, both secular and religious? While we cling to the labels of old, the puppeteers have their way with our world.

Where are common sense and clear-eyed journalism when you need them? Maybe the surprising rise of Bernie Sanders and Donald Trump in the 2016 election cycle indicates a deep, not just passing, dissatisfaction with the status quo political parties. Sanders articulated traditional liberal values, even though Democrats couldn't quite go there. Although the same can't be said of the megalomaniac Trump, he certainly did stir the ingredients in the GOP pot, with half of what he said pleasing conservatives, and the other half pleasing Republicans. Democracy is messy to make, but a terrible thing to waste.

One could and should of course make equally damning indictments of the so-called liberals and the current Democratic party. They are just as hypocritical and out of whack with their core principles as are the Republicans, although they are perhaps less dangerous to the future if for no other reason than their chronic ineptitude...an ineptitude that itself stems from the unmooring of principles through years of self-serving inconsistencies.

The only thing worse than a goddamn Democrat is a fucking Republican.

There is of course no definitive litmus test to separate differing political perspectives. Nor should there be. But the false polarities created by the confused bandying about of terms like "liberal" and "conservative" really do make it hard for reasonable analysis and governance. And that confusion, although particularly helpful to, and fueled by, right wing extremists, keeps our country tied up in knots in the early 21st Century.

We as citizens, and particularly the journalists among us, do not have to accept the co-opting of terminology and tradition. The Republicans can be whoever they as a party want to be. But I am simply going to call them Republicans because they don't deserve to be called conservatives.

Things have changed

For a more insider analysis from frustrated conservatives see the books *The Parties versus the People* and *Reclaiming Conservatism* both by former Republican Congressman Mickey Edwards; and *Goodbye to All That: Reflections of a GOP Operative Who Left the Cult* by Mike Lofgren, published in *Truthout 9/30/11*. For an erudite exposé on the clever and successful manipulation of terminology by Republican strategists, see the book *Don't Think of an Elephant* by George Lakoff, 2005.

Immortalized For Millennia... Mostly

Traveling around the eastern Mediterranean one thing stands out – or rather, doesn't. Everywhere time is captured here. Whether in ruins or local museums, one finds ancient, beautiful, hard, marmoreal statues, mostly of men and boys; realistic artistic celebrations of the body; a marvel of marble exquisitely formed by great skill and patience and with the simplest of tools. But no such statue I have seen anywhere near these Mediterranean Sea shores retains its genitalia intact.

Now I am sure exceptions exist (and the bronzes have fared better) and I've not been everywhere by any stretch. But I do get around and, as a man, pay a passing attention to such things. From my attentive, though incomplete, observations, the tally is: men made of marble – multitudinous; men made of marble with their penises present – none.

I do understand that some of these marbles still have their marbles, but near as I can tell, those were most all "removed" to institutions long ago. Removal is an act which when done by foreigners is called pillaging. One also may call it theft. The pillaging of patrimony continues as a hallmark of marauding hordes for millennia, whether they arrived by horse or Land Rover. Ironically, in retrospect, the looting and plundering may have been the saving grace for preserving some of the world's precious few marble genitals in situ. Based on historic observations one can presume that were it not for the laws and guards of major museums, the remaining few intact marble shlongs would find themselves victims of detachment by now too.

One cannot help but wonder what of this preserved treasure trove the Vatican has and what they do with it.

Maybe a few, wholly intact statues lie hidden under six feet of rubble, ruin, and centuries of silt. But something or someone has mutilated, castrated, or whacked off every statue I've seen. Let us dispense with a bogus postulation just to be clear. Did the sculptors make them that way? No way. The care and craftsmanship, the

artistic commitment, the most admirable symmetry all point to…
well, nothing but jagged edges where an apex of symmetry should
abide. So who did it, and did it so much? Maybe you can chalk a few
up to the fierce Amazon warrior women of lore with their hives
of enslaved men. I expect it would account for a fraction. If history
remains instructive and repetitive, the culprits were men. Men
who brought their own cocks to new shores and felt compelled to
commit a metaphoric insult as a punctuating attribute of conquest.
As if to say, "Your religion was wrong, your land is ours and now
your women need us, too." Perhaps it was a misplaced sense of
modesty projected onto a rock. Or maybe the marble one simply
looked bigger than their own and therefore they felt compelled to
destroy it. Any way you cut it, it is a pathetic shame. It doesn't take
balls to bust up art.

OVERPOPULATION'S PARADIGM PROBLEMS

A **frightening imbalance plagues** the relationship of humans with other species and natural systems, and the problem grows exponentially.

According to The Population Connection's statistics, eighty million people are added to the world's population each year, and the fifty poorest countries on earth are those with the highest birth rates.

The stresses on wildlife, forests, water, air and, yes, people, are amply documented, and no credible counter-arguments challenge the data. No one disputes the facts. Yet maybe the most important fact of all is that we continue to ignore the facts.

> *Many species of animals and birds have become extinct in the service of fashion fads, or fertilizer, or industrial oil. The soil is being used up; in fact, humanity has become a locust-like blight on the planet that will leave a bare cupboard for its own children – all the while living in a kind of addict's dream of affluence, comfort, eternal progress, using the great achievements of science to produce software and swill.* – Gary Snyder, A Place In Space (1995), p.39.

The collective impact of humans on this natural world defies sustainability. Our footprint is ubiquitous and obscene. If you simply look out the window of a plane the reality overwhelms. Human pressures distort natural cycles. And what does nature do when an overpopulation of anything occurs? Nature restores the balance, and the process usually isn't pleasant for those in the species receiving the adjustment.

The evidence glares if you pay attention from a non-hubristic perspective. Both science and common sense make the facts pretty much irrefutable. So why don't we take the matter seriously and try to resolve it? Why are we so quick to cop to denial? Or to feel helpless in the face of such an enormous challenge?

The intertwining problems appear thorny and knotty, creating a multi-headed hydra. Consider some of the elements of this equation, starting with this question: Why do people tend to have so many children?

Their religion tells them to, or at least they believe it does (e.g., "Be fruitful and multiply").

We are shackled by inadequate knowledge and available tools pertaining to birth control, and the knowledge and tools we can use are inequitably distributed to a staggering degree worldwide. Some religions obsessively compound this problem.

Poor people have historically felt a legitimate and understandable need to have large families for reasons such as high rates of infant mortality, providing for numerous "bread winners" in the family, and care of the elderly.

Our economic systems, in conjunction with our superficial value systems, conspire to persuade us to a lifestyle of consumerism. To make that system grow requires more and more consumers. (There must be a limit to how many TVs, cars and washing machines one family can use.) "Growth," "Progress," even "Success" are all loaded terms intended to feed the fires of consumerism. Adding more people to the process factors in as a taken-for-granted part of how it all works. We've all heard the phrase "the limits of growth," but dismiss it as an alien notion that goes against the current. No thinking person believes it a mere coincidence that those who champion unbridled growth are those who profit from it.

Here's Gary Snyder again:

> It must be demonstrated ceaselessly that a continually "growing economy" is no longer healthy, but a cancer. And that the criminal waste that is allowed in the name of competition – especially that ultimate in wasteful needless competition, hot wars and cold wars with "communism" (or "capitalism") – must be halted totally with ferocious energy and decision. Economies must be seen as a small subbranch of ecology...
> [p 39].

One more dimension lies hidden in this knotty equation, one most often discussed only in whispers. Here it is: If people who care about this overpopulation problem act responsibly and reduce the number of kids they have, the result will be a larger proportion of people in the world who don't care about the problem. If those educated about this problem self-limit their progeny, then the uneducated will become more of a majority. The knotty problem is also thorny.

So what logic provides the wise course? We have to do it all. None of these interconnected problems are insurmountable. They all arise from man-made human behaviors. But they strike us as intransigent for that very reason.

Religious leaders need to re-examine the theological exegesis which in earlier times served as an imperative to bring more children into the world. A giant, erroneous assumption permeated this flawed religious premise. There is no theological imperative or need to have more adherents. Perhaps the premise was based on raw numbers of adherents to put up against and prevail over other religions with fewer numbers. This understandable logic might have utility in a time without our current population pressures entering consideration. Inter-denominational clergy owe it to us all to talk intelligently about this out loud.

Knowledge and tools pertaining to family planning must become universally available and equitably distributed and accessible. Is this really such a hard thing for us to do?

The global community of humans could benefit immensely from a worldwide initiative on sustainable living. Among the most critical aspects of such a collective approach to living well are clean water, sustainable farming practices, and good schools developed throughout the world. If we significantly reprogrammed current military budgets, we could pay for this sea change of priorities. It could make a dream come true for billions. It would reduce the circumstances that lead to war by fostering good will and stability.

Many of the larger mammals face extinction and all manner of species are endangered. Natural habitat ("raw land") is fragmented and then destroyed ("developed"). The world's forests are being relentlessly logged by multinational corporations. Air, water, and soil are all in worse shape. Population continues to climb, and even if it were a world of perfect economic and social justice, I would argue that ecological justice calls for fewer people. The few remaining traditional people with place-based sustainable economies are driven into urban slums and cultural suicide. The quality of life for everyone everywhere has gone down, what with resurgent nationalism, racism, violence both random and organized, and increasing social and economic

inequality. There are whole nations for whom daily life is an ongoing disaster.
[Snyder on p. 46.]

We need to change our "growth" and "consumerism" paradigms into more sustainable designs. If we reassess our values, question the tricky enticements of consumerism, and shine the light of day on the math that plays out with unrestrained growth, we can make intelligent sea changes in how our children's children might thrive in this world. Easy to imagine. Hard to do. Better minds than mine will have to figure out, for instance, how a "social security" system would work in a more sustainable and well-considered model of human civilization in the world.

Most comprehensive and serious assessments of the problem of human overpopulation and its concomitant negative impacts on the natural world indicate clearly and with sound reasoning that we humans are headed for a fall. If the current trajectory is unsustainable, a remarkable change is inevitable... one way or another.

The matter will be resolved by a combination of horrible pain and creative intelligence. The proportions of each depend on how we choose to live in this world.

Thinking on Your Feet
with Your Foot in Your Mouth

I was working as a kind of jack-of-all-trades in a grocery store and one day while stocking the shelves in the Produce Department, I saw this guy coming down the aisle all dressed in a style I'd call Casual Perfect. He's looking like it's really beneath him to actually shop for food. In fact, I'm thinking to myself, this guy looks like he's got his butt hole torqued up so tight you couldn't push a raspberry seed up it with a marlin spike.

He walks up to me and says he'd like to buy half a head of lettuce.

I told him we didn't sell lettuce by the half head and he'd have to buy a whole one. He said he didn't want a whole one and insisted I cut it in half. I told him we don't sell lettuce that way, but he persisted so I said I'd go ask the Manager.

I walked into the Manager's office and said, "Some cheap idiot wants to buy half a head of lettuce," and I noticed the Manager was looking behind me with some concern. Glancing over my shoulder I saw the guy was right behind me so I quickly added, "And this gentleman would like to buy the other half."

We managed to satisfy the customer and later in the day the Manager called me in and said he admired how quick I acted on my feet, that he'd had his eye on how I work for some time, that he intended to open another store up in Thunder Bay, Ontario, and that he'd like me to manage it.

I said, "Thunder Bay? I don't want to go to Thunder Bay. There's nothing but whores and hockey players up there." The Manager's eyebrows raised up like the botox salesman had just walked in and he said, "My wife's from Thunder Bay," to which I replied, "Oh, really? What position did she play?"

SPECIALIST HITCHHIKERS

T he whole phenomenon started with a thumb. A local
reporter was cruising along U.S. Highway 2 on the north
coast of Wisconsin on his way to cover a story. He picked up
a hitchhiker who regaled him with tales of famous shipwrecks in
the Great Lakes.

When they got to the intersection where the reporter had to
turn off, they spotted a local bar and grill, as commonly found
at many rural Wisconsin crossroads. The shipwreck stories had
produced sufficient camaraderie to prompt them to go in for a
beer before they went their separate ways.

They got to talking and came up with an idea for the hitchhiker
to make a cardboard sign advertising his expertise as he continued
hitching rides. The reporter offered a side of a cardboard box he
had in the trunk and they made a sign right there on the bar,
which said:

RIDE TO U. P. – STORIES OF SHIPWRECKS!

The reporter was curious if the sign would work, so he ordered
another beer and took a seat by the window as the hitchhiker
went back out to the road. Almost immediately a car stopped and
picked him up.

When the reporter got back to the office he wrote it up as a
local feature story for the paper and ran it. The local NPR affiliate
saw it, called the reporter, tracked down the hitchhiker, and inter-
viewed them both on the radio. A photo went up on the affiliate's
website showing the geeky looking reporter and the hitchhiker,
who looked like a wildman, with both of them holding a mock-up
of the original sign. NPR ran the story nationally on a Saturday
morning, the web shot went viral, hitchhikers and commentators got creative and the whole idea took off into what became
a national phenomenon.

The middle class continues to shrink. The haves and have nots become ever more distinct. A burgeoning bouquet of reasons, most of them political, underly this trend. The trend is not abating. Out of these circumstances will come creative ways to ameliorate inequities. One of them will be an innovative way for someone with specialized knowledge or talent, but very limited means, to advertise for a ride. Someone with a car heading the same direction can select a rider with expertise in a subject of interest to the driver.

Imagine getting on the highway in Seattle for a trip to Portland. There, near the on-ramp under a long simple roof on the shoulder of the road, men and women are lined up holding a variety of signs according to their expertise. Imagine signs like these:

OCEANOGRAPHY
URBAN GARDENING
HISTORY OF BASEBALL
GEOLOGY OF PACIFIC NORTHWEST
COLLEGE FOOTBALL
ALTERNATIVE MEDICINE
JOKES
STORY TELLER WILL READ KEROUAC WHILE YOU DRIVE

Under such bold proclamations lies the name of the destination. Also coded on the signs might be an indicator of whether the hitchhiker could split the cost of gas, e.g., "1/2."

One would hope drivers rely on their eyes and intuition to determine who, if anyone, to pick up. Such personal informality far exceeds requiring hitchhiking permits that certify expertise and a clean record. Creating a hitchhiker licensing system would be intrusive, messy, and contentious. Yet we might as well get it on the table for discussion because some fearful politician and his or her constituents inevitably will suggest it. There could be regional rider websites where hitchhikers could post their information and even include a little resumé. Anything more structured stands as a bad idea deserving to die. Driver beware. Rider beware too.

While not exactly a sign of cultural progress, this work-around provides an accommodation to the less well-heeled. It levels the playing field a little bit by serving the mobility of citizens. For the hitchhikers, here's a way to use your skills to get around. For the drivers, you could think of it as a living version of audio books...

maybe a version that comes with gas money.

We round out this all-American story by tidying up some loose ends. The conservative curmudgeon who owned the paper fired the reporter for picking up a hitchhiker with the company car and contributing to making the news instead of merely reporting it. Within a year the reporter and the hitchhiker co-authored a book on shipwrecks, and the paper went belly up.

THE BIG CONVERSATION

All of the great organized religions of the world claiming to hold the literal truth are wrong. They are all man-made and they have all been corrupted or co-opted over time due to the desire for certainty, the zeal of leadership, the allure of power, the watering down that comes with being popularized over time, the ascendancy of rational linear thinking, and other human factors.

What I'm saying here is not to negate the intuitive, heart-felt, spiritual feelings and aspirations of people from all of the world's religions. To the contrary, I hope I am affirming the universal validity of those expressions in an important sense. None of us can know it all, but each of us who pays attention can sense the ineffable. We know something spiritual exists right here, right now, with every breath we take. I intend my words as an affirmation of the intuitive wisdom from which that ineffable sense springs.

I am, however, in a rough, bumpy, and very abbreviated way saying the trappings each of us is taught as a way of approaching the intuitive wisdoms are inadequate to the task as well as misleading. In fact, given how they have been manipulated and morphed over time, they are all now, in themselves, not worthy of belief. The idea that "God" abides somewhere else in Heaven nourishes the root of our misunderstanding, and excuses our exploitation of the earth and of life. It is a fundamental source of disharmony.

With a few exceptions, such as the simple experiential aspects of Vipassana meditation from the more or less original Buddhist teachings, the world's larger religions are confused and confusing. The great religions are, on a good day, sources of valuable and helpful myths and metaphors when understood in that context. But let us take a paragraph to explore the Vipassana example because it is a method of clean and simple spiritual exploration, albeit nowadays enveloped by an elaborate religion.

Vipassana is an identifiable and generally accessible spiritual practice aimed at wisdom which implies no hierarchies, no dogma, no belief, no faith, no surrender, no cultural baggage, no

preliminary requirements manda
claim of exclusivity, no mantras,
facilitate spiritual understanding
ential way. (This is not true of the
which encompass Vipassana.)

The Vipassana technique, so
or "mindfulness" meditation, is
unencumbered spiritual practice
practices found in various indig
deep within the larger, historic

powerful, eye-opening, and insightful. But for the most part they
are heavily barnacled by the belief structures within which they
are found.

So the question comes down to this: is life or reality intrinsically, innately sacred? Is it so without any human constructs such
as a Creator God, a personal God, a salvific code, and any other
trace of anthropomorphism? The answer is a resounding yes. Life
is sacred beyond the subjective---intrinsically sacred. The oneness
that underlies everything is that sacred essence. The manifesting
of this oneness (the creative force) is the expression of the sacrality.
Life is a holy event. God is a verb.

Life itself is so intrinsically interwoven with propensities and
creativities as to be worthy of the spiritual and wondrous word
"awesome." Life is profoundly beautiful and unpredictable (not
explained by a cold-blooded reductionism of science). I use the
word 'life' to mean all reality, to include everything---rocks and
water, as well as the dance of cause and effect.

The above truth can be glimpsed or gleaned through medi-
tative or other experience which produces the indescribable awe
of affirmation and humble respect. Reports of such experiences
come from all corners of the world, from all centuries from which
we have reports. Regrettably, too often these reports have been
interpreted or co-opted by the context of the prevailing religion
of the time and place.

The assertion that God is a verb, that life itself is an intrinsically
holy event, is not inconsistent with the highest reaches of scientific
observations and understandings. But it is awkward to agree upon
or even discuss, because science suffers from the same predispo-
sitions, language limitations, and anthropocentric tendencies as
religion...to say nothing of egos and other competitions.

ucible to a mechanistic (scientific) definition
ty is not entirely predictable, and values can create
es that act like particles? Particles that act like waves?
they come from and where do they go? There is more
an we shall ever fit within the bounds of our definitions.
evolved filters, languages, and other limitations keep us from
derstanding eternity is here and now.

Stuart A. Kauffman in his book "Reinventing the Sacred," a phrase he borrowed from Kiowa poet N. Scott Momaday, tries to get at such a holistic, sacred premise as a scientist and makes an important contribution to our conversation which has gone on for millennia. He gets a bit bogged down trying to explain the wondrous, multi-dimensional beauty of nature and what science is discovering about it. He is on the right track, but the articulation needs an injection of Taoist wisdom from Chuang Tzu and Lao Tzu, from iconoclastic poets like Rumi and Han Shan, from the Advaita Vedanta (beyond dualism) school of Hinduism, maybe some Meister Eckhart. A scientific inquiry would benefit from the reports of unfettered, non-doctrinaire mystics from many cultures and times, most certainly including indigenous wise men and women from everywhere. It could use a little Huston Smith, Joseph Campbell, Alan Watts, and a host of others too numerous to mention.

The question becomes not whether life is a sacred event, but rather, can we handle such knowledge without the weighty, contentious, constrictive, competitive baggage of all our inherited and accumulated isms? To prevent a moral anarchy, can we evolve from the purer knowledge of a respecting-all-life moral code or must we cling to the watered down, inadequate, and inaccurate dogmas?

This is an increasingly important question since the tattered, old, anthropocentric dogmas themselves are responsible for much of our despoliation of our planet and our violence toward each other. Given the increasing complexities and stresses we put upon life and its natural systems, and the exponentially growing potentialities of overpopulation, interconnected reliance on man-made systems, potential pandemic disasters, and increasingly powerful weaponry – well, we really should get past the lazy, convenient, self-serving ideologies of the past. To anthropomorphize a little, I think that is what life is telling us.

Eastern European Street Musings

Some people just know how to stroll. They make it look easy. Among all the thousands strolling this wide, pedestrian street in the afternoon sun on Good Friday, somehow you can spot the few Americans by how they walk: purposeful, rational, linear, destination oriented.

Some people dress to impress or entice. Others dress like they recently lost a bet, but who in the world should care? Frank Zappa once said, "Everyone in this room is wearing a uniform and don't kid yourself." Our serious self-images are kind of a funny thing. Camouflage riddled with transparency. And all so brief and changeable. Of many a couple strolling by, I can't help but wonder, 'What in the hell does she see in him?' Maybe someone looks at my wife sitting next to me and wonders the same.

> *Here you'll find no prohibitions yet*
> *against skateboards, cigarettes or dogs*
> *Some walk like Atlas*
> *some butterflies*
> *others like Sisyphus*
> *carrying the world*
> *in our different ways*
> *to the end of the long street*
> *to a perennial park*
> *where near a fountain*
> *chess is quietly*
> *a spectator sport*
> *under the canopy*
> *of an ancient tree*
> *that has heard it all*
> *for centuries.*

Thief of Information

I've been traveling internationally for fifty years – forty-seven different countries and about two hundred international border crossings. But today marks the first time I ever hired a guide to show me something. I am neither bragging nor complaining; it's just the way I've lived. I valued the economics and independence of doing it all on my own, but I missed a lot of once-in-a-lifetime opportunities to learn more about something or some place that stood in front of me.

So today, based on timely advice, we hired a guide to take us through Ephesus, Turkey. Ephesus…one of the wonders of the world. The place where Jesus' mother Mary came to live out her years after they killed her son. I learned more about Ephesus today than I would have on my own.

The people of Ephesus enjoyed tap water two thousand years ago, and made foreigners bathe before they entered the city. Baths on the outskirts of the city provided for that. They knew the world was round many centuries before the concept stopped scaring the hell out of Christians. Ancient engineers devised a way for the mosaic tiled floors of the homes to be heated by hot water flowing through pipes beneath them. Two long rows of sit-down style toilet seats stood in the men's communal john with a trough of running water beneath and live music in front. All this nearly two thousand years ago, just up the marble street from the world's third largest library—from which a secret tunnel ran to a brothel.

Much of what I learned I owe to Oscan, whom we hired to make learning easy and contextual. I came to appreciate the value of a good guide. I've watched these guides before, alright. I have seen them in action, and will confess right here I even sidled up to more than a few guided groups over the years to try glean some knowledge that peaked my curiosity about the Louvre, the Grand Canyon, the Taj Mahal… you get the idea. I made an effort to be inconspicuous in those moments, and not linger too long. But I did not pay the fair price, and watching Oscan's eyes today move toward an interloper tagging on the periphery of our valued lessons, I saw myself in previous places as a thief of information.

Fresh from the experience, putting on my best pseudo-guide demeanor, I gestured for my wife toward the stuffed, tooled leather, structured cushions as we passed the merchants' stalls and said, "These little gems from the harems of old were invented by the fierce Hassocks who were later overrun by the even fiercer Ottomans who took over the business and changed the name."

Other than spouting pure bullshit, I felt my presentation ranked as guide quality. I bit my tongue like a professional. I refrained from insulting the Aussies, those endless pursuers of linguistic reductionism who now refer to such finely crafted, traditional items as *"poufes."*

Talking About Antonin Scalia

Prologue: *In the time between the writing of this rant and when this book was published, U.S. Supreme Court Justice Antonin Scalia died. I consulted a number of people who had read the draft, and asked each of them if I should remove the piece from the book under the premise of not speaking ill of the dead. I was encouraged to keep it in. Most readers pointed to the gush of fawning accolades that appeared in the weeks after his death and insisted I should contribute to balancing the record of what was quickly becoming revisionist history. Another simply said, "Just change the verb tenses and go to press." That is essentially what I have done.*

Although Justice Scalia insisted vociferously he was a humble arbiter of judicial restraint, his snarky belligerence on that point was intended to cover up an opposite truth. He thrived on overruling Presidents and legislators. As the highly respected Supreme Court watcher Jeffrey Toobin pointed out in the February 29, 2016 issue of The New Yorker, Scalia helped gut the Voting Rights Act, overturn McCain-Feingold campaign finance reform legislation and in his last official act, blocked President Obama's climate change regulations.

If Scalia had prevailed in other cases, homosexuality could be a crime, same-sex marriage could be illegal, affirmative action would be illegal, key provisions of the Affordable Care Act would be unconstitutional, and women would have no right to an abortion.

One day in 2004 the Supreme Court of the United States agreed to hear the case of Judicial Watch, Inc. v. Department of Energy. It was an important case - important to the integrity of our democratic political process. The case involved the workings of an "Energy Task Force" created by President Bush to study and recommend the best energy policy for the country. Credible allegations had surfaced that the "energy task force" was a stacked deck; that the wealthy owners and directors of the oil and coal industries were controlling the process and thus the result, and that other interests such as clean alternative energy interests and environmental interests did not have an equal place at the table... to the extent they were included at all. A lawsuit was filed seeking release of the minutes of the meetings of the task force. Vice President Dick Cheney chaired the energy task force. He refused to release the minutes. The case made its way to the Supreme Court. On the line were the rights of the people to know what their government was doing.

Three weeks after the Supreme Court agreed to hear the case, while it was pending before them and as the briefs were being written, Supreme Court Justice Antonin Scalia climbed aboard Air Force Two with Vice President Cheney and flew off on a duck hunting adventure. An oil tycoon picked up the tab.

When this leaked out there was stunned outrage by people who give a damn. One of the cardinal tenants of our jurisprudence is that judges, all judges, should avoid not only improprieties but even the appearance of impropriety. This kind of extra judicial contact with a party having a case pending before the judge's court on a junket paid for by a party with vital interests in the outcome of the case was so far beyond the pale of judicial ethics that people questioned whether it was just a mean-spirited rumor, a lie intended to besmirch Scalia. When confronted with the question, Scalia smirked as he often did and feigned incredulity. Water off a duck's back. When pressed, he assured the public peons that there was nothing wrong at all, claiming that he and Cheney didn't share a duck blind or a bedroom – so what could possibly be wrong?

One can only sustain such arrogance successfully over time if one is essentially untouchable and has no conscience. It helps if you are also convinced that you are the very best living interpreter of the law and the U.S. Constitution. Scalia, possessed of all such factors, enjoyed himself quite smugly.

Antonin Scalia was appointed to the U.S. Supreme Court in 1986 by President Ronald Reagan. When he died he was the longest serving Justice on the high Court. He enjoyed a reputation of being gracious, gregarious, pompous, and intellectually slippery.

Scalia's self-described legal philosophy has two inter-related parts: "textualism" and "originalism". A textualist confines his review and application of the law strictly to the text before the court; most importantly the Constitution – what do the words say? Or if it is a statute, what do those words say? Scalia, as a textualist, purposefully avoided inquiring into the intent of the drafters of any modern law under review. He would not, for instance, consider the written, descriptive legislative history that accompanies the text of a new law. The principle of textualism is not without merit, but rigid adherence to it can thwart a search for justice and have a manipulative effect on the separation of powers among the branches of government. Originalism means interpreting the language (e.g., of the Constitution) as the drafters meant it when it was written. He was proud to say he simply and humbly carried on the awe and wisdom of the drafters, that he was perhaps the only one doing so correctly, and that there was no ego or bias involved in what he did.

Scalia said, "The Constitution that I interpret and apply is not living, but dead. Our first responsibility is not to make sense of the law - our first responsibility is to follow the text of the law." Here is an example of how such judicial philosophy works. When asked in an interview with C-Span in 2013 whether torture was unconstitutional, Scalia said torture is not punishment, torture is a way of extracting information from someone and anyone should be able to tell the difference. And since the Constitution only prohibits cruel and unusual punishment it doesn't apply to torture. He concluded by smiling and saying, "That's my view and it happens to be correct."

Brown v. Board of Education, the seminal case ending segregation, was decided before Scalia's tenure on the Supreme Court. When he was asked how he could support that decision when his "originalism" insisted on a "dead Constitution" interpreted through the eyes of the framers, many of whom owned slaves, Scalia had no good answer.

Scalia's clever, pushy arrogance disrespected the gravitas we entrusted to him as a keeper of the Constitution – for life. Speaking of life, a few years ago there was a last minute appeal to the Supreme Court of a death penalty sentence for a man named Troy Davis. Davis filed his appeal claiming he should get a new trial because there was new evidence which he argued could result in a different verdict. The majority of the Supreme Court agreed and granted him a new trial. But Scalia disagreed and wrote a dissenting opinion in which he said there is nothing in the Constitution that prevents an innocent man from being put to death by the state.

In calling himself an "originalist," Scalia would often say that means if you don't find a right specifically stated in the Constitution, then the Constitution does not give you that right, and you do not have that right unless the legislative branch gives it to you. Right to an abortion? Gay rights? Right to die? Nope. Not in there. Scalia would say, "You want a right to abortion? Pass a law." In other words, the government has to give us those rights. This, in spite of the fact the Declaration of Independence begins: "We hold these truths to be self-evident, that all men are created equal, that they are endowed by their Creator with certain inalienable rights…" To Scalia the Declaration of Independence carried no weight. It was superseded by the Constitution.

So if those inalienable rights aren't enumerated in the Constitution, then you don't have them. You have to ask the government to give them to you in a statute. That means any rights not considered by the Founders over two hundred years ago for inclusion in the Bill of Rights leaves any minority seeking protection subject to the "tyranny of the majority." This is of course exactly what the drafters intended to guard against when they wrote the Bill of Rights. They recognized that without the specific addition of the First Ten Amendments (i.e. Bill of Rights), not all citizens would have their rights equally protected, especially those with minority or unpopular interests. Important categories of rights needed to be beyond the political gamesmanship of the legislative process.

Such reasoning did not worry Scalia because as an originalist and a textualist he 'happened to be correct.' A highly abbreviated but still rather lengthy example of the effrontary and devastation such flippant abuse of power can cause occurred in a 1990 U.S. Supreme Court case called Employment Division of Oregon v. Smith. The case involved the right of Native Americans to use peyote in their religious ceremonies. A little background: according to anthropologists, indigenous people in the western hemisphere have been using peyote (a small cactus containing mescaline which has mild psychotropic properties) for religious purposes for 10,000 years. The oldest site evidencing its use in what is now the U.S. dates back 5000 years to the Simla cave in Texas.

In more modern times the documented use of peyote by Native Americans traces back to the 1600's and has grown since then into a pan-Indian religion with an estimated 250,000 Native people participating in the peyote rituals. In their all night ceremonies peyote is either eaten or drunk as a tea. In the early 1900's ethnographers from the Smithsonian Institution urged the members of the religion to create a legal church structure white men could recognize and relate to as a way to make sure the old, venerable way of worship was not destroyed by a misunderstanding of the legal system. So it happened that in 1918 the Native American Church was established under the law as a somewhat formal and recognizable religion. Life went on.

But in the late 1980's the state courts of Oregon were faced with a case where they had to decide whether a Native American had a right to use the peyote sacrament in the context of a Native American Church service. The Oregon Supreme Court said he did have such a right. They found the religion was protected under the Constitution of Oregon which guarantees the "Free Exercise of Religion," similar to the right in our constitutional Bill of Rights.

Unfortunately for the Native American Church, then Attorney General of Oregon, Dave Fronmeyer, was running for Governor on a "say no to drugs" platform and looking, of course, for juicy publicity. So he appealed his own state's Supreme Court decision to the U.S. Supreme Court. To the horror of church members, the U.S. Supreme Court agreed to review the case. In retrospect one can imagine Antonin Scalia licking his chops.

In the briefs filed in the case, and in oral arguments, it was shown that this religion among Indian people had been going on for centuries – even millennia before America was created (founded in significant part on the promise of freedom of religion). It was shown that similar cases arising in the Twentieth Century in state and federal courts had reached a conclusion similar to Oregon's. It was shown that this humble religion was sincere and not at all part of America's drug problem. The church's attorneys showed that even during Prohibition an accommodation was made to allow for churches to use alcohol as a sacrament.

In spite of all this, Scalia in writing for the majority declared extending the First Amendment's guarantee of free exercise of religion to protect the ancient, indigenous religious practice was, in his words, "a luxury our democracy can no longer afford." He stated the adherents of the religion would be subject to the ordinary criminal laws prohibiting drug use. Scalia and the concurring Justices turned a quarter of a million Native Americans into felons overnight.

After declaring the Indians would have no protection under the Constitution, Scalia rather dismissively wrote in his opinion if they wanted legal protection, they should go to Congress, i.e., entrust their fate to the tyranny of the majority.

This was in April of 1990. Although all seemed lost at the time, a core group of Native leaders and their friends and allies determined to try the congressional route. There was nothing to lose. Through a remarkable odyssey of four obsessive years, they were successful in getting Congress to pass a law specifically protecting the right of Native Americans to use, possess, and transport peyote throughout the United States in conjunction with the practices of their religion. I was proud to be on the core legal team of that four-year obsession.

Although in the end the result might be called a happy one for Native Americans, it should be noted it happened by the skin of their teeth in October of '94. The very next month was the election of Newt Gingrich and his class in Congress. Gingrich initiated the "Contract with America" bringing in the era of manipulative polarization which has spread exponentially to today's level of dysfunctional gamesmanship. It is almost certain that had the remedial law not been passed that month in '94, it could never have passed anytime since. Moreover, although there is such a religious freedom law in place, it is important to recognize that now it is just a statute and therefore subject to repeal or amendment. The protection afforded by the Constitution was stripped away by the pen of Antonin Scalia.

Although Scalia had no qualms about depriving Native Americans of their traditional religious freedom rights, he maintained an avowedly pro-Christian bias throughout his career. In a speech at Shearith Israel Synagogue in New York City he said in America neutrality on religion does not mean "neutrality between religiousness and non-religiousness but between denominations." One cannot help but notice his choice of the word "denominations" rather than "religions."

B ut he went even further. In a Ten Commandments case in the Supreme Court he said that the Ten Commandments are "a symbol of the fact that government derives its authority from God." Even more indicative of injecting his religious beliefs into America's jurisprudence, Scalia wrote in a "First Things" essay that unlike Europeans, Americans "are more inclined to understand, as St. Paul did, that government carries the sword as 'minister of God' to 'execute wrath' upon the evildoer."

While Scalia thrived on attention and controversy and laughed in its face, he did not want cameras in the courtroom. From his patronizing perch he said that "the people" just would not understand. There would be sound bites extracted and it would only confuse people. This from the man who continued to champion the Citizens United decision, where he said, "The more speech the better." When questioned whether that decision will lead to more misleading campaign propaganda, Scalia said the people will have to sort out what's true and what's not. Of course, when questioned further he said the "Free Speech" language of the First Amendment does not specifically require us to show our court proceedings to the public on TV... just read the original text.

In the wake of Citizens United, the multi-billionaire Koch brothers have a recruiting effort to get the captains of industry to fund right-wing infrastructure for front groups, political campaigns, think tanks and media outlets. Among those in the secret network of Republican donors were Supreme Court Justices Scalia and Thomas. As Bill Moyers said, "Two of the five votes (in Citizens United) to enable the final corporate takeover of government came from Justices who were present as members of the plutocracy hatched their scheme for doing so." (See www. thinkprogress.com for more.)

T o many judges, legal scholars, attorneys, and other serious believers in the Constitution – in particular the role of the Judiciary – Antonin Scalia was a terrible tarnish. In our times when the bar of integrity in government continues to lower, it is reasonable to expect Scalia's example will not only be followed, but built upon.

Scalia was smart. And clever. In combining those qualities he was a world-class bullshitter. I would encourage everyone to look for interviews with him and listen closely. He was slicker than snot on a door knob.

One last thing, admittedly speculative. The demographic trends in America are irrefutable. In a few short decades white people are going to be in the minority. Wealthy white power brokers actively work to consolidate powers in such a way that their interests will be so institutionalized, so ingrained in our social fabric, that even though they lose numbers they will still have a certain amount of control. If you look at Scalia's actions in many, many cases, including Employment Division v. Smith (religion) and Citizens United (politics), it is fairly compelling to connect the dots.

So what could we have done about Scalia? Almost nothing. He was insulated in one of the most powerful seats in America for life. No recall. No term limits. No recourse.

But there are a couple of interrelated things we can try to do. We can shine a light on the man. Deconstruct his cultural manipulations. Expose his smug hypocrisy. Show him as the scary clown he was. And one more thing: vote for Presidents who will not appoint another sanctimonious prick like Antonin Scalia.

The Tonner Club

Some have asked me not to print this story because of its offensive nature. The story challenges norms, but has the virtue of being true.

The story concerns an unusual club I learned about years ago while studying for the bar exam. The young man who revealed the story was also studying for this exam. He and I were in law school at the same time, but had not really met until the exam process found us in an intense, temporary, and transplanted circumstance in another state. Due to the demanding nature of the bar review course, there were occasional episodes of stepping away and goofing off for an evening. One such night we made our way to a Middle Eastern restaurant featuring a belly dancer. Maybe it was the respectful comments about the dancer's wonderful body that precipitated the tale he confided. Whatever it was that got him talking, he presented the story with a strange combination of confidentiality and enthusiasm.

While he studied as an undergrad he somehow became part of a group of guys who called themselves the Tonner Club. This rather discreet little group of young men, as I came to understand the story, was an ongoing group – in other words members would come and go while they were students and graduated, but the Tonner Club concept would continue with incoming inductees, in this regard much like other college clubs.

But the Tonner Club was in most other respects unique. It had a very simple premise. To become a full-fledged member, one had to have sex with enough different women whose total weight equaled a ton, two thousand pounds.

Two important requirements fell within this undertaking. The first was simply that one could only count each woman one time in cumulating his total. The second rule was the kicker, each woman had to weigh a minimum of two hundred fifty pounds.

You can immediately see why you may never have heard of this club, no matter how many years you spent in college. Not much is commonly known about the Tonner Club, and what I know comes second hand, from the tall, thin, confidential source who assured me he was an accomplished member in his day. Moreover, he convinced me of his sincerity, and provided some detail. The most common denominator of all the successes seemed to be alcohol, the primary lubricant of casual sex. But as much as alcohol may have facilitated both participants in lowering their inhibitions and getting it on, there were other quite interesting aspects to the encounters.

As sexist as the whole enterprise may sound, life turns in curious ways. My source confided in almost all encounters, the big woman was an enthusiastic and passionate lover once they got in bed, often for her the first time with anyone other than herself.

There followed, of course, in latter conversations, jokes among club members about getting lost in the folds of flesh and, are you sure that you were where you thought you were? But with a big-eyed, beaming smile my confidant told me how unexpectedly enjoyable such romps became because of the energetic sexuality of these big, fat women. He described respectful, reciprocal (albeit brief) relationships. He said you could never tell the woman their tryst began as a Tonner Club pursuit. He said you would never want to appear so crass, especially since the sex was passionate and delightful.

Rather, he said, each encounter was an adventure in pushing one's limits, an adventure in both seduction and understanding. In listening to him I got the clear sense he felt he was a better, more compassionate person for having undertaken what initially seemed like a crude and superficial adventure. I imagine him now a long married family man. I cannot imagine his wife. Well, I can, but...

Before leaving, I asked if he thought there might also exist a female equivalent of the guy's Tonner Club. He looked wistfully off into space and with the hint of a smile said he had no clue... but he believed it would be a good idea.

Midwestern Train Station 2009

The Amtrak station in Portage, Wisconsin, in 2009 stands much like more rural train stations in the Third World, in the sense that the train often arrives late and you will find no one to ask how late. But differences quickly appear. In the Third World there is always some place to go to the toilet, and an electric light so one could read a book. Did I mention you'll find neither food nor water here? Pretty unlikely not to encounter a vendor or two with food and drinks at a train station, even a rural one, in the Third World.

On the Portage siding, there sits a small, dark shelter on the platform consisting of four walls, a roof, and some two-by-four benches. Right near it lurks a big old railroad building which formerly housed both the passenger and freight station. But these days passenger and freight trains are separate corporations, and freight has the building, along with right-of-way on the tracks.

The large freight building is locked tight and on each door it says Employees Only Beyond This Point in big, bold, fearful orange letters. Inside the well-lit rooms you can see vending machines and bathrooms. A railroad man comes out of the freight building and I hurry over to ask about my late train. Without looking at me he says, as if for the hundredth time, he works for Canadian National, the freight corporation, and doesn't know anything about Amtrak. Doesn't know why it's late or when it's likely to arrive. He hastens to add that no one inside knows either and they don't have a way to find out. And finally, in response to my last question, he ends the conversation with, "No, you can't use the bathroom. Can't you read the sign?" He goes back inside and closes the door.

After peeing on the platform, I return to the little passenger shelter in the growing darkness. The only sources of information are the four No Smoking signs (one on each wall) and the large No Smoking Policy Statement which is three paragraphs long. It concludes with a toll free number and website, in case you want more information about the no smoking policy.

I took a seat in the dark and made up a little tune.

If I was a smoker
and I had smokes
I'd be smokin' now

FROM VIRTUOUS TO VICIOUS

By the early 1970s times were changing in the USA. The civil rights movement had made a huge difference in both access and attitudes across most of the country, some changed by persuasion, some statutory, and some driven by court decisions. The health, safety, and wages of working men and women were also in the ascendance. Environmental concerns were finding a prominent place in public policy discussions and in legislative and regulatory actions. I thought the future looked brighter. I thought America was maturing. I was damn near optimistic. Those were heady times.

But not everyone was turning the same corner. What some of us saw as progressive, others saw as alarming. Among them was Lewis Powell. Powell was an influential corporate attorney and had been President of the American Bar Association. Two months before President Nixon nominated him for the U.S. Supreme Court (on which he served 15 years) Powell wrote what was essentially a manifesto. It was 1971. He called it a memorandum. It was lengthy, detailed, strategic and alarmist. It was addressed to the U.S. Chamber of Commerce and also sent to the Captains of Industry. The title is "CONFIDENTIAL MEMORANDUM: ATTACK ON AMERICAN FREE ENTERPRISE SYSTEM."

Powell laid out the case for business to wake up and take action. He looked at those advances in civil rights, labor laws, and environmental protection as tremendous threats to business interests. He called on business leaders to wake up, organize, and take action to turn the tide in favor of unbridled capitalism. He argued in detail how the progressive gains hurt commerce, and business leaders should control the agenda of America's future. It was a political call to arms to American business leaders.

Powell of course wasn't alone. His grousing about the ascendancy of civil, labor, and environmental rights was already going on in board rooms and country clubs. But after Powell's Memorandum, greed was good again. In the American dream, money talks and business has the money. Or, put another way, the Golden Rule was increasingly interpreted to mean, 'He Who Has the Gold Makes the Rules'.

I found out about Powell's Memorandum and how it led to a tipping point by reading "Who Stole the American Dream?" by Pulitzer Prize winning author Hedrick Smith. The book was published in 2012 and includes Powell's Memorandum as a 21-page appendix.

The urgency of the message outlined in Powell's manifesto caught on with business leaders. They ponied up and hired pro-business lobbyists to influence legislators, spent their advertising dollars to influence media, used their donations and business leverage to affect pro-business changes on college campuses, hired attorneys to cherry-pick cases to create pro-business court decisions, and doled out yet more money to lobby for the selection of pro-business judges. Private business and industry have led an increasingly sophisticated and successful fight to gain and maintain control of American law and policy.

Few people criticize short-sighted self-interest and greed these days. In fact, those characteristics are now rewarded because they describe the people who make the laws and set the policies. As resulting social problems inevitably arise, the rich persuade the middle class to blame the poor.

We are in the fifth decade of the slow-motion hijacking of the American dream. Time to take a look at some of the damage, but first let us revisit the economic practice that sustained a large middle-class without requiring two or three or four sources of income simply to keep a family healthy.

Economists call this pattern the "Virtuous Circle of Growth." The behavior is characterized by a strong middle class keeping pace with changes in the cost of living and thereby causing money to circulate through society over and over again, nurturing everyone equally along the way. Egalitarian principles keep money recycling in messy circles of growth. Such principles are based on an equitable tax code, support for manufacturing, fair electoral rules, and balanced regulatory rules for safety. All of these factors were skewed toward the rich in recent decades, as we shall soon dissect.

Thomas Jefferson said, "Manufacturers are now as necessary to our independence as to our comfort." But something happened after Powell's Memorandum. The aggressive greed that was organized and unleashed in the years since has dramatically shifted the focus of the Virtuous Circle away from the people doing the work and toward the stockholders in the companies and corporations. Employees get short-shrifted so owners and CEOs can maximize profits to shareholders who then vote to raise CEO pay. It results in a much diminished Virtuous Circle of Growth, an exponentially increasing concentration of wealth at the top, and the off-shoring of jobs and manufacturing in the interest of corporate profit. Industry and production in America shrivels.

There is a longstanding American policy and practice of spurring growth through government and private partnerships. Examples include the Erie Canal, the railroads, the highways, the moon project, the telegraph, the Internet, and GPS. But these days oligarchs invoke the romantic myths of rugged individualism and pure capitalism to brand any such projects as 'socialism,' insisting the word is pejorative.

But it doesn't have to be this way to have a progressive modern society. Since 1985 the wages in Germany are up 30%; in the U.S., 9%. Germany has a two trillion dollar trade surplus. The U.S. has a six trillion dollar trade deficit (2000-2010). In Germany 21% of the workforce is in manufacturing; in the U.S., 9%. All this is due to Germany's social contract bringing together business, labor, and government for the nation's benefit.

A merican industry has touted and promoted the international trade agreements as good for our export markets. In large measure it is a lie. The agreements allowed corporations to move overseas for cheap labor and corporate profit, all at the expense of American working people. The off-shoring cost not only jobs, but the fluid interaction of innovation and production. Equally outrageous in its hypocrisy is the confession of some CEOs that they save more money on their investments in China through Chinese government subsidies and tax breaks than from Chinese cheap labor.

The Reagan and George W. Bush tax cuts saved the super rich one trillion dollars each decade, with very modest benefits to the middle-class. Wages used to keep pace with productivity. A roughly level playing field was maintained by adjusting the tax code and labor laws for that purpose. The top tax bracket under

Eisenhower was 92%; 77% under Kennedy. That was an era of steady economic growth (the Virtuous Circle of Growth). Today the highest tax bracket is 35%, not counting loopholes.

Speaking of loopholes, the current corporate tax code, which favors off-shoring everything, resulted in General Electric making 10.5 billion dollars in profits from 2008-2010, but instead of paying taxes they got a federal tax rebate of 4.7 billion dollars by using loopholes and claiming tax credits.

Tea Party supporters have pushed hard and successfully on tax-related issues. I say "supporters" because they are not creating their own agenda. Tea party voters are more akin to puppets than free-thinking individuals. The clever few at the top have duped people into aggressively pursuing ideas against their own interests. Over half the members of the House Tea Party Caucus are millionaires. On average they are twice as rich as other House members. Their tax strategy, led by Grover Norquist, calls for privatizing Social Security, eliminating welfare, cutting defense, education and farm subsidies, aid to the disabled, at risk youth and early childhood development, and selling government facilities such as airports. Norquist and his power broker backers have cajoled 238 House members and 41 Senators into signing a pledge to never raise any taxes. They have also cajoled thirteen governors and 1,249 state legislators. Pathetic. All these pledges are nothing more than manipulated bravado, for our tax revenues are at their lowest levels in sixty years, and the U.S. has the third lowest overall tax rates of the twenty-eight most advanced economies in the world.

Warren Buffett paid 17.4% in tax on his 2010 income, the lowest rate of anyone in his office. If you're making money with muscle, sweat, and hard work, your tax rates go up. If you're making money with money, your tax rates go to the lowest level. Buffett recommends repealing George W. Bush's tax cuts for the super rich, imposing a higher tax on those making over one million dollars a year and an even higher tax on over ten million a year.

We also could tax corporate stock options, which are a hefty slice of the obscene largess given to corporate officials. And we could amend the payroll tax rules that say the super rich pay no payroll taxes on any of their income over $106,800 per year. The biggest and simplest idea is to end the 20% capital gains tax rate and instead tax investment gains at the same rate as wages and salaries, which is 35%.

There are so many inequities, so many simple solutions, and so little political will. It is both a national embarrassment and a national tragedy we the people allow ourselves to be so exploited when, in fact, our democracy empowers us to do better. Pathetic. A relatively good political system wasted on Americans.

In **2003, more Americans** filed for bankruptcy than had heart attacks. More filed for bankruptcy than got cancer or graduated from college. More filed for bankruptcy than for divorce. The top 1% of income makers in the U.S. make more money annually than France, Italy, or Canada. The top 1% got two-thirds of all economic gain in 2007, then 93% in 2009.

And yet we fall for the romantic myth of unfettered capitalism. Even though forty-eight million Americans get sick each year from tainted food and three thousand die, the Tea Party Republicans push to cut millions from the FDA budget for overseeing the safety of the nation's food supply. They also oppose funds for retraining Americans thrown out of work because their former employers moved overseas. Oh, and did I mention Tea Party Republicans oppose the government providing disaster assistance after hurricanes? Just to be clear, I mean hurricanes in the U.S.A.

And yet somehow these same selfish, myopic dupes are gung-ho for increasing the defense budget. "Fuck you, Grover," I almost hear them say. After the Korean War Eisenhower cut defense spending 27%. After Vietnam Nixon cut it by 29%. After the Cold War Reagan also cut it, as did GHW Bush and Clinton. George W. Bush raised defense spending by $200 billion a year. Obama raised it, as well, one of the only things the Republican Congress would agree to during his administration. In the 2016 presidential primaries all the Republican candidates except Rand Paul stumbled over each to see who could raise the military budget higher than their opponent.

According to the Eisenhower Study Group from Brown and Boston Universities, the Iraq and Afghanistan wars will cost four trillion dollars. Let me just add this to that: historians remind us "Imperial Overstretch" has been the downfall of empires. Domestic budget shortfalls and their ensuing problems, and war power increases (think fear mongering and sabre rattling) devastated Spain in the 1600s and England in the 1900s. Amen.

This would be a good place to slip in a plea for ending the idiotic and undemocratic process of gerrymandering – yet another example of how democracy is wasted on Americans. Gerrymandering is roughly the power of the majority party in a state to draw the boundaries for the voting districts that will select representatives to the state and federal legislatures. The crazy quilt configurations they arrive at typically remain in place for ten years. The practice thwarts democracy. One can only wish it was beneath our dignity. Here are some examples of the results, which are good indicators as to why all the problems discussed above remain intransigent:

Republicans won a thirty-three seat advantage in the House, even though more people voted for Democrats than Republicans;

In Pennsylvania Democrats outpolled Republicans, but the Republicans won thirteen of eighteen seats;

In North Carolina the Democrats won the popular vote, but the Republicans won nine of thirteen seats;

In Michigan the same story, but Republicans won nine of fourteen seats;

It's not just the Rs. In Massachusetts and Connecticut the Republicans won one-third of the votes, but got zero seats in Congress.

So where are we? Well, we're right here in the middle of the nest we keep shitting in. Most people are working longer hours for a smaller piece of the pie. Most people are voting for bad governance. The oligarchs and plutocrats are convincing them to do so with cowboy notions of rugged individualism and Ayn Rand aggrandizements of unbridled capitalism. It's the unraveling of the woven fabric of a cohesive nation. It's the hijacking of the American dream. It is the vicious tumor of greed devouring the Virtuous Circle of Growth.

In the Soviet Union, capitalism has triumphed over communism. In this country, capitalism has triumphed over democracy.

– Fran Lebowitz

PRONUNCIATION GUIDE FOR SPEAKING FRENCH – WITH A MOUTHFUL OF 'FREEDOM FRIES'

The following brief and simple primer is intended as a pragmatic guide to describe in plain English how one may try to communicate with the French. It does not attempt to address the more troublesome question of why. I provide examples and cultural references where they might prove helpful. So let's begin with some basic elements of how to pronounce words in French.

As a general rule, when speaking a French word you should pronounce the first consonant you encounter clearly but lightly. Any consonants you subsequently encounter as you progress through the word simply hint at – as if they were perfume. As you gain proficiency, you can begin to ignore them entirely.

Whether other, more consonant rich cultures in Europe claimed a disproportionate share of said consonants early on, thereby leaving a dearth for the French, is a matter of some historical debate, a knowledge lost to the French in the mists of time, much like their ingenuity. It's not that the French don't have consonants. They do. They just can't articulate them, much like their values... with the exception of promiscuity.

Some have even posited that the French purposefully eschewed consonants, especially the hard consonants, similar to the way they avoid hard decisions, thus making it a cultural trait distinguishing them from other peoples, much like their body odor.

Moving on to the vowels. When appearing in the first half of a French word, vowels should be blurred together, but by the end of the word they should be pronounced only as an airy smear of vowelish sounds, flowing mostly from your nose. It is helpful to think of French vowels as if they are made of fresh watercolors and your voice as a very wet brush.

The French, to be sure, are more than generous with their vowels, sometimes insisting on three or four in a row even when the resulting sound is achieved in other languages with a single letter. For instance, "O".

The French take great pride in their language, which is understandable given the paucity of other original cultural attributes. Be that as it may, they are very protective of their world-renowned baguettes, and you can't take that away from them – unless you're a McDonald's franchise.

The French deserve great credit for their uncommon clarity in telling the U.S. to go fly a kite in Iraq, but damn their eyes for the residual messes of their colonialism. For example, they imposed their limp lingua on the fine country of Morocco, thereby creating a handy post-colonial playground of a surrogate, cultural treasure trove.

Regrettably, only French speakers can pronounce half of the rich cultural beauty they expropriated with their lingua franca. The frogs fuzzied up a linguistic world in Morocco where both the Berbers and the Arabs respectfully pronounce each and every valued letter in their own languages. In that gorgeous land even "th" consists of two distinct sounds, which I discovered checking into the fine, old Batha Hotel in Fes.

The reader may wonder if I exaggerate in attempting to offer practical advice for the usage of French consonants, vowels, and word construction. I would only suggest the examples corroborating my assertions are very many ... or should I say, beaucoups?

INDIAN MASCOTS

I'm a white guy, so I'm going to write this with the pronoun "*we.*"

First we conquered them. With military might and fortified by the Christian church we stole their land. Took it for ourselves. Over time, with lies, greed, and deception, we took their languages, their religions, even their children through policies and laws we forced upon them.

We created an inevitable trauma among Native people, from which they are now recovering. Then, to add insult to injury, we made cartoon caricatures of them for our amusement. We expropriated elements of Indian cultures and turned them into shallow shams, as if they have no meaning. We claim it is not demeaning because it celebrates wholesome athletics, team spirit.

Bullshit.

We make these cartoon mascots symbols of the games in our stadiums, eerily reminiscent of the arena battles hosted by the Roman gladiators for their own amusement...and to convince themselves of their good and superior life.

There is a cruel and tragic aspect of human nature that makes nearly everyone, every group, desire to have someone, some group, lower than themselves. One way to do that is to turn them into caricatures of who they really are.

By depicting another culture in such a way, we don't really have to take them seriously, we don't have to acknowledge the damage done. We can feel good about ourselves; buy a ticket to the arenas in which Native people are rarely present.

The Washington Redskins? How about the Cincinnati Jews? The Minneapolis Mexicans? The Boston Blacks? The New York Kikes?

Ask yourself this: why are Native Americans the only living group we dare to insult in public?

On Making a Trail in the Woods

There's nothing worse than going into a nice stretch of woods and finding it to be a jumble of man-made trails. All the natural depth and mystery destroyed or imperiled by a maze of ill-considered tramplings as if a committee of drunks went in there to lay out a motocross course.

On the other hand, a well-considered, simple trail lets the magic hide in the deep mystery that is the woods. On such a path you and your fellow creatures know you walk in life's journey. So before you go making a destructive mess which will take old Ma Nature and all her four-legged friends tons of energy and years of time to repair, please give some thought to the following observations.

Having a chance to make a trail through the woods presents a rare and wondrous opportunity. Approach it as the creation of a work of art, because that's what it is. The woods are your canvas, your page. The trail, your brush stroke, your poem. A trail comes alive for many good things: for animals, for health, for pleasure, for posterity, for learning, for movement, for beauty. Approach the making of a trail with the same sense of responsibility as if you were building a home for your family. And let's be clear – these woods do not belong to you. No matter what the chain of title says and how much you pay in taxes, you arrive at best as a temporary steward in a long and patient history. Avoid saying "my woods." Practice saying "these woods." And you should also avoid saying "my trail." Better to say "this trail" because more animals and even plants will make use of the trail than you could ever possibly know. Animals appreciate unimpeded movement and a better view of potential dangers. Seeds and pollen are transported with less obstruction, and the openness allows for new growth. The trail provides a gift to the woods and the things of the woods.

Take your time. Don't make it in a hurry, and don't design it with a goal of traversing it in a hurry. Trail making holds more important considerations. I used the word 'design', but really making a trail unfolds more as an act of discovery than of design. The trail must fit the woods. It should look like it belongs there and has been there a long time.

Begin by spending time in the woods. Quiet time. Move through and observe the woods at different times of day, from very early to very late. Even in different seasons if you have the time. These are reconnaissance missions. They are vitally important because the trail you make must be in the right place. Making too many trails is one of the worst things you can do to the woods. A trail should lie in the woods like a simple, elegant necklace on an attractive, intriguing woman.

Begin to see where the trail wants to go by seeing where the animals have made their trails. Theirs are trails of life and death. Trails of evolved thinking. Evolved trails. Trails informed by the principles of chi and feng shui.

Because these principles are so central to our trail work, let's take a moment for a layman's look at what they mean, with apologies to the masters.

Chi. Consider it the energy of life itself. Think of it as vitality on a subtle level that flows through everything. You know how some places and circumstances just seem to drain your energy even though you're not doing anything strenuous? How other places and circumstances give you a sense of well-being, like your spirit has been nourished a little? That's the ebb and flow of chi. It's real and it's everywhere.

Feng shui. Consider it the art of placement, of the relationship of objects to each other in space; how you can move through that space with harmony and efficiency and appreciation; how everything seems in its place, nothing is superfluous, and nothing is in the way. That's good feng shui. The ingredients and characteristics complement each other and invite you to their best use, facilitating your intended purposes. All this in a way that makes you feel good, enhanced, at your best, relaxed, and replenished with chi.

Many often apply the principle of feng shui to the placement of objects in a room (furniture, mirrors, lights). In our case the woods got here first and the forest furniture (tress, bushes, rocks, shadows, contours) was arranged long ago by Mother Nature. So our task is to move ourselves, via the trail, in a way that employs the principles. Animals, especially larger ones, may have already done much of this, but their interests do not entirely coincide with ours.

So in our reconnaissance phase we must look not only for animal trails but also for unique objects and views. Things to celebrate, make note of, things that make you smile or feel intrigued. The fine, found art of the forest. The trail need not go right up to its wonderfully signature features, but if possible it should provide an opportunity to see them along the way. Whatever fits.

After all this homework is done, it is time to rough out a trail. In this phase, as well, you must take care to disturb as little as possible. Proceeding along a course you think may be the right one, loosely tie some bright ribbons to limbs or stems to mark a 'maybe' trail. Put them like bread crumbs within easy eye sight of each other as you go. When you get to the end, turn around and go back again.

Be mindful of some other basic considerations. Is the trail too straight or too curvy? Does it accommodate nicely various uses that may apply, such as cross-country skiing or elderly people walking? Don't be afraid to move the ribbons. That's the reason for tying them loosely. Use your intuition. And leave the ribbons where you last put them.

Now go away and come back another day. Applying all the same considerations and techniques go back and forth on the 'maybe' trail some more. If you can't think seven generations ahead, at least imagine how everything would look in a hundred years. Age the woods in your mind's eye as you stand back and as you walk. Do this in different light, at different times of the day. Do it over several days or many days, if you can. When you've finally travelled the length twice in both directions without moving the ribbons, it's time to go back and get the best tools needed for the job of clearing the trail.

Clear the trail. Take your time. As you go if you uncover a particular spot with an inviting view and good energy (a chi spot), consider putting a bench there, facing just the right way.

A trail can expand wide enough for two abreast where it wants to, single file where it fits. Don't force it either way. No need to make it too wide, but do plan for plant encroachment because the woods has a longstanding habit of fully occupying itself, and it will try to reclaim the territory, no doubt about it. But don't over-worry, the woods will respect your trail…to a degree…over time… if the trail runs in the right place.

If time and circumstances permit, you might consider doing something akin to the old Native American trail practice of using "Indian Marker Trees." An Indian marker tree is fashioned by purposefully bending a sapling and holding it in a bent position through most of its young life. The horizontal portion indicates a direction, or boundary, and the upper portion then resumes skyward. This marking technique is most appropriate if the trail is long and contains a juncture from which it's not obvious where to go next. The technique of indicating a direction, or perhaps a boundary, acts like a natural road sign and has a long lasting benefit.

We've come to the last consideration: low maintenance.

Low maintenance is key to happy trail enjoyment. A natural ease makes and keeps the trail inviting. Pick up a light stick and use it to flick little branches off the trail as you go. There will always be a little maintenance because that's the way Mother Nature operates, as she sprinkles the forest with long time nutrition and protection. A bit of tidying up is just part of a good walk, more of a curiosity and an opportunity to learn than a chore, and different every time. An old well-formed trail is always new, like a river. If you pay attention, you never walk the same trail twice.

Bonus: Consider finding a tree, dead or alive, with a crotch or knot hole in it. Plant it near the beginning of the trail. The crotch or knot hole is a place to put your worries and woes before you take the trail. You won't need them on your walk, and after you've traveled the trail, you can go back and pick up those old troubles… if you want to. I learned this from a wise, old Omaha Indian named Elmer Blackbird. Elmer died with loving kindness in his heart.

OF LAWS AND PRISONS

Part I: The Rule of Law. Imagine you are walking down the road of life thinking about how fleeting and relative it is on the one hand, and how precious it is on the other, and you hear your name called for jury duty. It's a horrible case, one that in some state and federal courts the accused, if found guilty, could be sentenced to death. Imagine you are in one of those states.

Most countries don't have the death penalty. Among those who don't are all of Europe, Canada, Australia, and Mexico. Among those who do are Afghanistan, North Korea, Iran, Syria, Saudi Arabia, and the U.S.A. More than one hundred countries, according to Amnesty International, have abolished the death penalty.

Within the U.S., eighteen states have never had the death penalty or have gotten rid of it. In the other thirty-two, state-sanctioned murder remains the law of the land. In recent years there have been thousands of cases of exoneration where, through DNA or other exculpatory evidence, the convicted person was discovered to be innocent. Some of those were death penalty cases. We have no way of knowing how many innocent people remain stuck in jail, and especially how many innocent people the feds or the states have killed, and we will never know. But if that number exceeds zero we should weep. It is safe to assume the number is significantly greater than zero.

Imagine being summoned for jury duty in a death penalty case. Here you sit, one of a large pool of prospective jurors. Attorneys for the prosecution and for the defense are interviewing all the prospective jurors in a process called voir dire, trying to narrow the pool down to a dozen, with perhaps an alternate or two to wait in the wings. Central among the questions posed to the prospective jurors is whether you are neutral and open-minded and could go either way on the question of voting for the death penalty, depending on the facts of the case and how they fit the laws to be applied in determining whether or not the death penalty is appropriate. Or are you biased for or against the death penalty?

Suppose you are deeply, morally opposed to the death penalty. Your heart, your mind, and your gut tell you it is simply and truly wrong for the government to kill someone through an intentional process. It is abhorrent, uncivilized, and reprehensible. It goes against your best understanding of spiritual teachings, your informed code of ethics, and what your mother taught you.

Now you have a dilemma. You can certainly affirm that you are capable of finding the person on trial to be guilty if that's what the facts lead you to believe. And recommend severe sentencing. But what about recommending someone be killed?

There are conflicting, maybe irreconcilable, ways of looking at law and jurisprudence. Knowledgeable, ethical and thoughtful people have told me that in this circumstance you must confess your bias in order to preserve the integrity of the judicial system. This view holds the viability of society depends upon each of us playing by the rules, adhering to the law, supporting the system we have created, without injecting our own qualifiers into the mix.

But there is another perspective from which to view the law. This view makes those of the first perspective nervous and fearful of anarchy - anxious the fabric of society will come unraveled. Fair enough. That is a legitimate concern. However, I don't think it is dispositive because of the following assertion: most people are going to abide by the law, play by the rules. Life is riddled with fuzzy edges to everything. If you or I determine that our moral compass compels us to color outside the lines on some issue, so be it. Tough beans for the majority's code. If the social fabric can't tolerate a few loose ends, maybe it needs to be rewoven anyway. But that's damn unlikely.

This second perspective on the law sees the law as a patchwork of human construct. It was collectively created primarily as reactive responses to human foibles, follies, and bad acts. As such it is merely the lowest common denominator by which we have agreed we can get along. It is not particularly lofty.

But lowly patchwork that it is, it is still the glue that holds societies together. Seeing the legal structure as something lofty or almost sacrosanct is a collective myth we, mostly, share as a way to elevate the law and compel adherence. Our man-made laws are a house of cards compared to nature's laws. And as such we invest extra clout in the collective myth of our laws' inviolate nature. It is why courts get so incensed when you violate their orders, because they fear it threatens the whole enterprise. A proof the enterprise is man-made and, therefore, tenuous is revealed in the fact that defying court orders is considered more egregious than defying the original law which got you into court in the first place.

It might be true if each of us followed our own moral code rather than the law, we would quickly descend into social chaos. I think humanity as a whole is capable of such selfishness and bad manners. So in this sense I'm content to see everyone else adhering to the collective myth we hold as the nobility of the law. I acknowledge tuning my ear to a different drumbeat fairly relies on most everyone else adhering to the rule of law...which they seem content to do. Therefore, I'll just go on about my life trying to abide by what I consider loftier principles, such as the Golden Rule and its twin sister, Common Sense.

This means, in our hypothetical, I would be willing to deceive the court in the voir dire process into thinking I was neutral as to the death penalty if that meant I might be given an opportunity to save someone from being killed by the state.

Part II: Prisons, Penance and Apathy. In our self-described "Greatest Nation on Earth" we take law and order seriously. You step out of line in the "Land of the Free" and we'll lock your sorry ass up according to pre-established mandatory formulas written by people of privilege. Seriously.

We like to have a few progressive "pilot projects" going on here and there which are more holistic, somewhat thoughtful and require a little more heart and brains. These "experimental programs" are tolerated when they arise in a community possessed of a little more heart and brains. We tolerate these bright spots because they are rare. For the most part we're pretty sold on the black and white of law and order and the "out of sight, out of mind" results.

According to the Pew Center Study of 2008, one out of every 100 Americans is in jail on any given day. One in 30 from ages 20 to 34. One in nine blacks in that age group.

Nearly six million of us have lost the right to vote due to criminal convictions. In some states one out of every four blacks is barred from voting.

There is no way this is good for democracy. On the participatory democracy side of things, six-hundred thousand ex-felons in Florida were denied the right to vote in the year 2000. That was the year of the paper thin margins giving Bush a "victory" over Gore and thus the presidency. Not only did their uncast votes not count, but their disenfranchisement did. And how do you get meaningful "prison reform" laws and policies when the folks who know the system from the inside are precluded by law from voicing their vote? Instead, we spend increasing billions in a way so out of whack that in some states we spend more on prisons than on higher education.

We have the highest incarceration rate by percentage of population in the world with a very few very creepy exceptions. It is a national embarrassment. And speaking of creepy, consider this: the demographics of America are irrefutably changing such that in the coming decades people of color will be in the majority. Threatened, the people currently in power (read "white") are taking what steps they can to consolidate and preserve their power. Disenfranchising the prison populations, who are disproportionately people of color, plays into that strategy – as of course does disproportionately arresting and sentencing them in the first place.

In addition to the political impact of our out of control policies, are the even more profound personal impacts on the lives of the incarcerated and their families. People come out of jail stigmatized, ostracized and rendered almost unemployable by the combination of receiving no skills training in the slammer, followed by the humiliations of constraints and bullying by punitive probation officers. Add to that the taint of admitting to a prison record on job applications where disclosure provides nothing relevant.

We need to champion alternatives to incarceration and mandatory sentencing. Young people commit most crimes. They make dumb or immature mistakes. What would you want to happen if it was your kid? You would want those in charge of the system to use their hearts and brains. What really happened? Why did it happen? What were the underlying causes? How can we remedy those? If there was a victim, what does the victim want to see happen and how can that be worked out? What does the person who committed the wrong want to have happen in his or her life? What dreams and skills? Can we find training or mentors or other help here to get this person on a healthier track? How do we make the whole thing accountable, and thus mitigate against repeating bad behavior?

These are just some of the basic questions that come from an application of principles rooted in The Golden Rule and Common Sense. They are the questions and principles applied in traditional cultures for millennia to restore balance when someone acts out too far or goes haywire.

Some people simply have to go to jail. This is not the rant of a Pollyanna. Civilized society must remove some people from the streets and the public. Some perhaps for the rest of their lives. It's been that way for a long while in a lot of places on earth and it looks to continue for as far as I can see.

But it still leaves plenty of room to design what incarceration can do with and for people. We've slipped in our thinking in America. Never did get it right, but we have only gotten it worse. We are far too quick to simply warehouse prisoners in whatever bare bones conditions our courts will allow under the Constitution. And of course the trend toward privatization of prisons exponentially increases the problem. Too many vested interests in the current system. Too much power and money exerted by the "prison lobby" to continue to feed the beast. Here's how it works: those invested in private prisons (mostly white people) lobby their elected officials (mostly white people) to be tough on crime, pass more punitive laws, keep the masses under control, increase funding for the prison industry, accept their campaign contributions, and oh by the way, if all this results in certain "demographic groups" having reduced voting power, well, let's just call it a fortuitous, unintended consequence.

By using our hearts and minds instead of emotions and formulas in dealing with people who cause trouble with the law, we can shrink the stresses of overpopulation in our jails and prisons. This alone would provide some breathing space to make the institutions more civilized.

Instead of only punishment spartan warehouse style, wouldn't we all be better off if jails and prisons focused on higher principles of penitence and rehabilitation? Penitence means regret for one's wrongdoing, contrition - clearly an appropriate goal for a penitentiary, has the same root word. Rehabilitate means to restore to a good condition – another appropriate, noble, and civilized goal.

It is important to acknowledge some jails and prisons do offer a few programs both to give credit where credit is due and to take away the cheap shot of dismissing the larger point by asserting I am uninformed. And yet, those educational or healing programs make up a tiny fraction of what could occur. If we focused our use of incarceration as a teaching and healing opportunity for a captive audience, we could change the fate of most prisoners and thereby of society itself since most of them return to our communities.

Consider this: a prison where inmates are encouraged to participate in skills training (trades, crafts, arts) where the system provides literary workshops, meditation courses, stage plays, true libraries and schooling, sports, gardening, farming, cooking, welding…

An equally important counterpart to those programs should be mental health services – counseling and treatment. According to the U.S. Dept. of Justice in 2014 more than half of the prisoners in the U.S. have mental health problems. Our country now houses three times the number of mentally ill people in jails than it does in mental hospitals (NY Times, The Week, Feb. 21, 2014).

The statistics alone make it inescapably obvious our present system is uncivilized. It means we are routinely making moral errors in the judicial processes of prosecution and sentencing. As a result the best we can say is the troublemaker has been taken off the streets. The bar lingers far too low. By simply applying cookie cutter formulas of statutory application, all too often including "mandatory minimum sentencing," we remove a troubled soul from our midst and put him or her in a hellish cage. Out of sight, out of mind.

Why can't we tailor solutions to problems? There is no good reason we can't provide more quality attention at the front end with considerations of treatment options, restorative justice, counseling, penance, or what have you, which fits the circumstances. Everyone knows whether you're building a house or a car or a family, providing more quality of attention and the proper tools at the front end saves magnitudes of trouble, maintenance, and expense in the out years.

Investing in fertilization produces better fruit trees. Investing in education produces better citizens. By precisely the same logic, investing in people in trouble and in troubled people, produces healthier people and a healthier society.

Since plain incarceration is so expensive, and since it accomplishes so little, and since recidivism is rampant and even more expensive, why don't we look at people's bad acts more holistically and address them with more compassion and creativity? Is it not likely the increased costs at the front end would be more than justified by the savings in the long term? And wouldn't it make us more civilized? Isn't that a value to embrace creatively?

Free market capitalism contributes heavily to these conditions, yet does nothing of its own accord to address them. To the contrary, the prison industry encourages increasingly punitive policies and penalties.

Where are the religious leaders on these matters? And where are those who believe in their religious teachings? Where are the mental health professionals, the secular humanists, the social scientists, the journalists? We should all feel ashamed.

"The worst sin towards our fellow creatures is not to hate them, but to be indifferent to them; that's the essence of inhumanity."
– George Bernard Shaw

Why shouldn't we, as a society, be doing all this? Do we have something better to do as a society? Isn't it in everyone's best interest? Isn't it the civilized thing to do? Recidivism rates are very high, sometimes over fifty percent. That should tell us a couple of things. First of all, our prisons release inmates who are unprepared and unwelcome in society, marginalized, stigmatized, alienated. Secondly, we're sentencing ourselves to the high costs of incarcerating repeat offenders...and creating more victims in the process.

Fear and funding are the factors which compel us to uncritically continue to increase our support of the current growing prison systems. This is low thinking and works like a myopic knot. We increase problems and then we have to deal with them... reactively and expensively. It is some kind of pathetic we don't demand more of ourselves and our systems. And it's apathy. We hide behind tired old adages - "an eye for an eye," "out of sight, out of mind." A very pedestrian logic persists that because someone commits a bad act, society should punish them, period. An eye for an eye.

And once we have justifiably locked them away we can forget about them. Out of sight, out of mind. That is lazy, reductionist thinking. How can we claim to hold life so precious, even sacred, and be so callously dismissive?

The shame an offender might feel, upon examination, next falls on us.

Note: see *When Brute Force Fails*, by Mark Kleiman, pub. by Princeton University Press, 2009.

THE PROS AND CONS OF NAMING THINGS

Many learned men and women have identified the distinction between "rational/linear" thinking and "intuitive/cyclical" thinking. Rational/linear thinking traces back to the Greeks, first credited with developing and championing the power of such an especial way of looking at the elements of life – particularly natural objects and events, in their component parts and in discreet isolation to the extent possible. This manner of thinking works well as an efficient process of managing matter.

In this way the Greek technique of cognition became the dominant modern Western, and increasingly worldwide, thought process which has led to an astounding amount of knowledge and facts, and the resulting manipulation of nature to serve the needs and desires of humans. Just think what we've done with medicine, the wheel, the harnessing of energy, mass production and distribution of goods and services. Profoundly powerful.

Indigenous people worldwide, on the other hand, are credited with developing intuitive/cyclical thinking. As the designation suggests, this method of understanding is more relational, more referential to the turnings of natural cycles, more inclusive and holistic. You could say intuitive/cyclical thinking is more humbling and less hierarchically judgmental, focusing instead on the interconnectedness of all life. Being alive in this world view is not limited to things that breathe or move, or other rational, technical definitions. Here rocks are alive, just like lightning or water or the sun. Here humans are not the boss... not even the presumed wisest form of life. Here humans are less likely to have individual advantage, and more likely to live simply.

On the other hand, along the rational/linear way humans are more likely to disrespect and even contaminate their world. Rational/linear thinkers do not accept the validity of principles such as "what goes around comes around," or Karma. They are not restrained in exploiting nature for immediate, logical purposes. This results in an anthropocentric belief in the unbridled myth of human progress, which exponentially increases the possibility of the collapse of major man-made systems - the very systems upon which we are increasingly dependent.

Rational/linear people are arguably better at collectively creating more personal comfort and wealth by manipulating or exploiting the natural world, but individually they lose some resilience. They become somewhat out of touch with the basics, with nature. Rational/linear people rely on heat and hot water at their fingertips, but may be incapable of building a fire.

Intuitive/cyclical people remain better at sensing and understanding their place in the great scheme of things, less demanding, more tuned into the natural tumblings and humblings of life, less reliant on comforts and therefore more resilient. When the power goes out, who stays the warmest?

In the event of major breakdowns or collapses of the systems we make and rely on, one would be much safer and more likely to survive among indigenous thinking people. To carry the thought out, in such an event modern America stands out as perhaps the most dangerous place in the world if the major systems upon which we depend collapse. Modern Americans quickly become flummoxed and helpless if they cannot turn on electricity or running water for even a day.

In retrospect, it is not a coincidence that the old, Greek manner of thinking caught on and resonated in the West. The Abrahamic religious perspectives have much in common with rational/linear thought, perhaps because those religions and cultures emerged from the desert, a relatively stark, black and white environment. Judaism, Christianity, and Islam all share the same roots in the dualistic precepts of right and wrong, good and evil. These religions have man at the center of a linear path where time is conceptualized as finite, with its necessary beginning and end. The compelling logic of rational linear thinking gives Christians their pushiness; Muslims too.

On the other hand, the indigenous ways of perceiving life have more in common with Eastern perspectives coming from more complex landscapes; perspectives such as Hinduism, Buddhism, and perhaps, most strikingly, Taoism. Eastern religions are less homocentric, less exclusivistic, and include a profound cyclical path of rebirths for all of creation, where matter and energy transform in perpetuity, where time has no specific or necessary beginning or end.

To my mind Taoism in particular is basically an indigenous spirituality that just happened to develop an early written component and, therefore, got included among the so-called "historic" religions with Hinduism, Buddhism, Judaism, Christianity, and Islam.

Ironically, from the far reaches of rational/linear thinking we learn reality does not quite fit within the boxes of our definitions. We discover light might be a particle or a wave or both. That matter and energy can neither be created nor destroyed. That matter consists primarily of empty spaces. That some plants are more like animals and some animals more like plants. We learn from the creative edge of science what the mystics have long asserted: not a thing has its existence within the bounds of our definitions. Nature has fuzzy edges. Nothing exists in isolation from everything else. You can't capture reality with names.

And yet naming things in isolation gives power. Categorization and deconstruction are the processes by which we manipulate or exploit nature and natural systems. But naming things dismisses their relational value. It is reductionist and allows us to treat things as isolated and impersonal – without inherent value. A recognition of the inherent value of the interrelatedness and interdependency of all aspects and elements of life is essential to holistic understanding.

Holistic understanding is represented in the Eastern mystical sensing of a tapestry of life beyond individuation. In such a world we view life as more mysterious, more awesome (in the spiritual sense of the word) and we live in the realm of interconnectivity.

For centuries, the Lakota continue to sit in a circle on the ground singing and praying for "all my relations." For centuries we hear stories of the Zen Master responding to his student by pointing silently at the moon – not because he doesn't know the name, but because he knows so much more than the name.

The late Vine Deloria, Jr. (Lakota) said the following in response to a question about the difference between the Western and indigenous ways of life:

> *I think the primary difference is that Indians experience and relate to a living universe, whereas Western people – especially scientists – reduce all things, living or not, to objects. The*

implications are immense. If you see the world around you as a collection of objects for you to manipulate and exploit, you will inevitably destroy the world while attempting to control it. Not only that, but by perceiving the world as lifeless, you rob yourself of the richness, beauty, and wisdom to be found by participating in its larger design.

(as quoted in *The Sun*, July 2000, p.6)

Fortunately, rational/linear people are beginning to realize the interconnectedness of the world in which we live. Unfortunately, nature had to hit us over the head with extreme weather, rising temperatures and surging sea levels, and rapid extinctions to get our attention. Perhaps we can turn the tides of our own creation, so that our world begins to get better faster than it gets worse.

RAMBLING ON I-80 IN NEBRASKA

Speeding east squinting into the morning sun headed home. Out here where the nation's breasts are named Country and Western and water has no rights. Enjoying a stone alone daydreaming of my family and the sacred nature of nature. Rolling plains and bad policies everywhere you look. A nice home and a few trees are worth their weight in gold, and we need better government than we deserve. Since people have piles of paper claiming they own the earth, you'd think they'd dummy up and care. Sometimes America seems like an ignoble experiment – Earth as petri dish for our reckless disregard. And sometimes I am light with awe. The hours go past like the "original pony express" station in southern Nebraska. Heading back to the Rez in late July, nearly pow-wow time. Wanting to go fishing with my beautiful son and yet somehow far easier to believe in what I do for a living than to go fishing... or pay the rent. This highway teems with characters same as history – rock crushers and skinheads, billboard gluers and tree surgeons, new friends and influenced people, movers, shakers, sleeping beauties, white bears, broken glasses, all kinds of bandages on all kinds of sleeves, people happy to be alive and a few dead ducks, lovers bouncing along in trucks, people who talk nasty,

there's a fellow in the other lane
one hand on the wheel and one on his brain
mirrors on his rain soaked windows
dark eyed desperados slinking home, sad eyed senators racing away, horse's tail in a trailer door, horse's ass in the slow lane. Vintage footage of America on Parade. What can this fellow be thinking sneaking up behind with a lady in his lap? Looks like he's going as fast as he can, when he should be slowing down.

Road builders, body builders.
rock 'n roll busses rolling in a row
highway full of misfits

bikers and bankers
at the wayside stopped to think
some hurried some worried
some faster than stink
the bitch in the station
is looking most glum
the bearded kid by the bridge
has a sunburned thumb
cartoon beaneries and dog fights
muskrat guts and headlights
the Platte looks wide and inviting
from a speeding car
whole families on the riverbank
being as they are
truck driver looking down a fat lady's dress
making the pass that he knows best
the boys in the back of the school bus
are mooning the teacher's van
everybody's moving approximately
as fast as they can
salt and pepper sideburns
orange and purple hair
the highway is a theater
gallon of gas the fare
with cruise control and self control
and variations on a theme
weaving in and out of
each other's dreams.

In a stereophonic 3-D roadshow the sun went down behind me, the highway rolled on without me. I turned down a little winding, gravel lane toward home. And an hour later my daughter was conceived.

PEACEMAKING

One night "Johnny A," for no good reason, winds up spray painting some graffiti on an old lady's house and happens to get caught. He has to go to Juvenile Court where the judge is told this isn't the first time Johnny's been in trouble. He's had a few other minor run-ins with the law and up till now the authorities have been lenient. He comes from a broken home, and his record at school shows he is uncooperative and has a bad school record. Lots of absences, a couple of fights, and poor grades in most classes. His mother has attended a few parent teacher conferences and a couple of disciplinary meetings with principals and counselors. The record shows that things have gotten progressively worse at school. The Juvenile Court is at the point where it gets serious. The number of incidents, the lack of measurable improvements, the crowded court docket, and the commitment to treating all delinquents equally means that this time Johnny A is court ordered to a Juvenile Detention Facility in another county for a period of one year. There he will be housed and attend classes with other juvenile offenders in a quasi-prison facility enclosed by a double row of security fences topped with razor wire.

One night "Johnny B," for no good reason, winds up spray painting some graffiti on an old lady's house and happens to get caught. His case is brought before a judge who is concerned about what is happening to Johnny and orders that the matter be sent to a Talking Circle. A circle is convened by a facilitator. It includes the facilitator, Johnny, his parents, his grandparents, a school principal and counselor, the old lady, and, if appropriate, a spiritual leader with whom the family has a connection. They all sit in a circle of chairs. The facilitator opens the session while holding a Talking Stick. He explains the process and then hands the stick to the person on his left. Whoever has the stick can speak. You may not speak until you have the stick. The stick is passed around the Circle for as long as it takes to reach a good conclusion. When the stick is passed to you, you can say whatever you want or nothing at all and pass it on.

As the Talking Stick goes around the Circle a fuller picture emerges. Johnny's dad abandoned the family and provides no support, and, in fact, once told Johnny that Johnny would never amount to anything, a point that has stuck in Johnny's mind. Johnny often is late for or absent from school because too often his mother has a new "uncle" at the breakfast table so Johnny won't come out of his room. Yet, although he is falling behind in most classes at school, he really shines in shop class, and did the finest work with wood in the whole class.

As the picture unfolds and the Talking Stick goes around the Circle again, creative ideas begin to emerge to address underlying problems and help get Johnny back on a good path, sustainably and accountably. Dad apologizes for saying terrible things he doesn't remember saying and commits to being supportive with time and money. Mom did not realize her boyfriends made Johnny feel ashamed and, with her parents watching from across the Circle, pledges to change her ways. Someone points out that the old man across town, famous for making wooden boats is getting feeble and could really use a helper. The old lady, after all is said, simply wants her house repainted and an apology. She offers to buy the paint and says her nephew will help Johnny with the work. Johnny is contrite. Someone finally listened. He begins to trust the offers of support which respect him as a young man, and he accepts the responsibility that goes with it, including repainting the old lady's house and becoming a helper to the boat maker three afternoons each week. Perhaps someday Johnny will apprentice with the boat maker.

The facilitator writes up the Agreement. Everyone in the Circle signs it and it goes to the judge to be entered as an enforceable Order of the Court. The strong likelihood is the court will not have to enforce the Agreement/Order because the parties themselves crafted the Agreement and are mutually invested in its outcome. In the event of a breech, the Circle can be reconvened. In the unlikely event the entire process collapses, the Order of the Court remains and the adversarial process waits in the wings.

Johnny A lives in modern America. Johnny B lives in an indigenous community which has not traded in its old ways for the modern adversarial system. Or, perhaps more likely these days, Johnny B lives in an indigenous community which is experiencing the re-emergence of traditional justice.

Traditional justice systems have evolved all over the world for millennia with wonderful and profound variations. In the U.S. such a variety of indigenous justice practices tends to come under the general heading of "Peacemaking." When I first learned of these practices from a group of tribal judges, I said, "Oh, sure, you mean Alternative Dispute Resolution, ADR," to which they replied, "Oh no my friend, we're talking about Traditional Dispute Resolution, TDR. That adversarial model you imposed on us – that's Alternative Dispute Resolution." My eyes opened and my respect deepened.

The intent is not to solve an immediate problem through the application of uniform, neutral laws, and regulations. Rather the intent is to resolve a disharmony, to address problems holistically, to restore balance to an individual, a family, a community as the case may be.

The traditional justice or peacemaking approach is front-end loaded, as the stories of the two Johnnies illustrates. It requires more time and energy from more people in a participatory way. That is not to say no one cared or tried to help Johnny A. No doubt the family tried in their way, schools tried in their way with their rules and resources, and others, too, may have offered on their own what they could to Johnny A.

But in Johnny B's case all the relevant energy and information was brought together in a more inclusive and holistic way. There were fewer underlying unknowns, fewer loose ends, fewer avenues of avoidance or buck-passing. Humanity evolved with Johnny B. The system integrated more factors, making the approach more comprehensive. Johnny reduced the odds of his defiance escaping the process and rising up again.

One of the most common and effective ways of engaging in peacemaking comes to life with the use of Talking Circles, as was the case with Johnny B. Variations of the Talking Circle have been around for millennia throughout the world. That alone should tell us quite a lot. In recent years a growing body of literature on Talking Circles is coming from anthropologists, social scientists, and peacemakers themselves. A good sampling of them follows at the end of this essay.

Consistent reports describe the phenomena called "the power

of the Circle." It is the manifestation of the whole being greater than the sum of its parts. Circles often take on a life of their own. There are no dark corners in a circle. Everyone is equal and sitting on the same level. The presence of all the relevant people in the Circle creates a revealing web of pertinent ingredients including facts, emotions, principles, compassion, reason, history, goals, humor, and creativity. A wisely run Circle brings out the best in people through the dignity of a respectful process. Put another way, it is using the Golden Rule to arrive at common sense.

One of the contemporary peacemakers of some renown was Dorothy Davids, known affectionately by hundreds and perhaps thousands as Aunt Dot. Aunt Dot was an elder member of the Stockbridge-Munsee Band of Mohican Indians, and she had a reputation as a powerful peacemaker, though she might say she really didn't do much at all. When Aunt Dot was asked to facilitate a Talking Circle to address persistent and tenacious disputes which might be intra-family or inter-family or just between two individuals, she would often begin by asking the parties to the dispute, "So, what is it that you like so much about fighting?" This simple, pointed, and often unexpected question had a way of shaking people out of their attitudes, messing up their defensive positions, and opening doors to a healthier future.

Peacemaking is not for everybody. But it is for most everybody who is intelligent and emotionally mature. However, there are some people who, at least in some circumstances, will insist on getting their pound of flesh. People who insist on rolling the dice in the adversarial judicial system. In such circumstances peacemaking has no use for them. The central parties to a conflict must be willing to give peacemaking a chance.

I once had the opportunity to join a team of teachers leading a course in peacemaking at the National Judicial College in Reno, Nevada. The teaching team and the class consisted almost exclusively of tribal people, with me being the only non-Native in the room. During the course of one session I mentioned that modern western mediation teachers told me mediation is typically ineffective in domestic violence cases, because of an imbalance of power in the relationship. In their view, the deck is too heavily stacked by one side to allow for an equal playing field in which both parties could find a mutually agreeable resolution.

Several deeply experienced and wizened Navajo women

peacemakers looked at me with increasing attention. Finally, they challenged what I said. Not true in their peacemaking, they offered. Bring us those cases, not a problem, we'll level the playing field!

Tribal peacemakers will tell you one of the strengths of peacemaking is personal accountability. They point to the relative anonymity one can hide behind in a majority society's adversarial process where a judge who doesn't know you addresses your problem in a courtroom isolated from your world. One peacemaker I know tells the story of sitting as a judge in a tribal court and a young man comes in on charges of domestic violence as a repeat offender. The judge, feeling exasperated by the ineffective procedures his tribal court had adopted from the adversarial model, told the young man how things were about to get different. The judge said the young man was going in front of a panel of elder women in the tribe to explain himself. The young man was scared shitless. He begged the judge not to do that. He said he would plead guilty and to please send him to jail. The judge did not relent.

The young man indeed did appear before a group of elder tribal women. No one knows what happened, but the peacemaker/judge now gives a beaming smile when he recounts that this fellow, still in the community, has not been in court in the several years since the peacemaking session.

Just as peacemaking approaches are front-end loaded in terms of investments of time and energy, the adversarial model also has its downsides. This we see especially in the criminal context where our society struggles with crammed court systems and burgeoning jail and prison populations, not to mention their increasing costs, including those trends associated with the privatization of prisons. In some states the costs of incarceration now exceed the costs of education.

On a more subtle level the litigation model is based upon a reliance on laws, rules, and regulations because those are the elemental standards upon which the adversarial process works. It is the application of strict written laws, regulations, and procedures which govern the disposition of cases. Of course through time it results in an increase in the number of laws, regulations, and procedures due to ever-changing circumstances and societal pressures. An increased fear of lawsuits has arisen from the resultant litigation. Since the law is supposed to treat everyone equally, the result of a previous case serves as precedent for the next. Call it fear of the cookie cutter.

One can see why peacemaking works better than litigation in places such as Indian reservations, small towns, and rural counties. In such places one cannot hide in anonymity, and the people are shaped by their interrelationships. In litigation we rely on an equation of winners and losers. When the gavel falls, one side walks out of the courthouse feeling they got justice, perhaps smugly, and the other side feels they got beaten, perhaps angrily. In smaller societies adversarial results are a real problem because of the variety of ways in which the parties may be interrelated – through family, church, neighborhood, employment, marriage, civic projects, ethnicity. Creating winners and losers through local litigation sends negativity into the air. Disharmonies arise which create conditions such as isolation, factionalism, bitterness, and other complications which make life more difficult and less pleasant.

The case for using peacemaking as an alternative to litigation and the adversarial system in large cities might be tougher to make than it is for smaller areas. In more urban areas the interrelationships are more diffuse. Anonymity serves as more of a buffer.

The case for favoring peacemaking becomes stronger when factoring in the financial costs. Although the Peacemaking approach to resolving disputes arguably requires a larger hands-on investment of time at the front end, the financial costs are dwarfed by the expensive adversarial litigious model with its vast-expenditures on court related costs in both the civil and criminal arenas. This is especially true when adding all the costs related to incarceration, including juveniles and repeat offenders.

The time and expense of appeals and the costs of enforcing court orders also eat up resources. When a judge imposes a final ruling, who can blame a disgruntled party for appealing if they feel wronged? Why not roll the dice again? Additionally, the enforcement of judicially imposed court orders often burdens the system for similar reasons and/or because of more pragmatic problems the court may not have considered.

With peacemaking such court-clogging and deeply frustrating problems typically do not exist. The reason is simply because the parties reached a resolution, refined and agreed to by the parties themselves. As tribal peacemaker Dave Raasch (Mohican) puts it, "Who is going to appeal peace?"

Peacemaking is not too good to be true. It is not a magic pill. It requires the skill of the peacemaker and the commitment of the stakeholders. But it can certainly work in many, if not most, cases. It is not a coincidence that variations of peacemaking are found in indigenous cultures worldwide. Peacemaking brings out the best in our holistic thinking and comprehensive problem solving. It is a path with dignity on the road to sustainable harmony and the preservation of cultural values. Peacemaking is life-affirming.

Here are some sources for more information:

The website of the Native American Rights Fund has a substantial bibliography on Peacemaking on their website (www.narf.org) – some of the articles below are linked to that Peacemaking page.

Life Comes From It: Navajo Justice Concepts, by Hon. Robert Yazzie, 1994, New Mexico Law Review, Vol. 24, No. 2, p. 175ff.

Returning to the Teachings: Exploring Aboriginal Justice, by Rupert Ross

Peacemaking in Your Neighborhood, by Jennifer Beer

Peacemaking Circles: from Crime to Community, by Pranis, Stuart, Wedge

Mediation Quarterly, Special Issue: Native American Perspectives on Peacemaking, Vol. 10, No. 4, 1993. Editor Diane LeResche, Ph.D.

Strengthening Tribal Sovereignty Through Peacemaking: How the Anglo-American Legal Tradition Destroys Indigenous Societies, 28 Columbia Human Rights Law Review, 235, Robert B. Porter, 1997.

To Set Right Ho'oponopono: A Native Hawaiian Way of Peacemaking. The Compleat Lawyer (ABA) Fall, 1995.

Yuuyaraq: The Way of the Human Being, Harold Napoleon, 1996.

The Reawakening of Sacred Justice, Diane LeResche, 1993.

BEWARE OUR THEOCRATIC "FAMILY"

What you are about to read is half rant, half book report. Jeff Sharlet did our nation an important and eye-opening good turn by writing the stunning exposé called, "The Family, the Secret Fundamentalism at the Heart of American Power," published in 2008. Sharlet is associate professor of English at Dartmouth and a contributing editor for Harper's Magazine and Rolling Stone.

This story exposes a group of people, many with familiar names, called, "The Family" or sometimes, "The Fellowship," committed power brokers working and praying in secret about what they call a "Spiritual War" to bring "Biblical Capitalism" to the whole world. This is free-market fundamentalism, part of an "imperial ambition" undertaken not in the name of Christianity, but in the name of Jesus – or as they like to call it, "Jesus plus nothing."

The Family describes itself to itself in a profoundly simple way. They are motivated by love from and obedience to Jesus and that's it. Jesus plus nothing. The theology of Jesus plus nothing is totalitarian in scope, but diplomatic in practice. It doesn't conquer, it infects.

As we will see in these pages, The Family consists of Senators, Congressmen, captains of industry. They are a creepy elite who believe their success proves they are God's chosen people, mandated to transform the world…and not in a direction you may want to go.

The Family declares God's covenant with the Jews is broken, and the core members of the group call themselves "the new chosen." These people are Dominionists. They believe God chooses everything, and in the name of Jesus they feel obliged to reconstruct the world to the way it was immediately after Jesus, when his teachings stood pure and unencumbered – before the creation of the Christian church and its dogmas. People with power have power because God gave it to them. Therefore, they have a responsibility to remake the world in Jesus' name.

In the words of former U.S. Senator Mark Pryor (affiliated with The Family) "Jesus didn't come to take sides, he came to take over." To The Family the word "Christian" is a term they deride as too narrow for the world they are building in Jesus' honor. They rise as "followers of Christ." Faith or kindness does not drive them, but obedience, as they understand it, to the person of Jesus. As their highly revered elder leader Doug Coe puts it, "There is nothing in the Bible about the Christian church."

They often quote Romans 13: "The powers that be are ordained by God." They don't particularly care about individual sin, they care about salvation understood in terms of nations becoming "the Promised Land."

The Family is a self-described network of followers of Christ in government, business, and the military. They consider themselves a core of men responsible for changing the world. They belong to an invisible network quietly working its will for over seventy years. It includes traditional fundamentalists, evangelicals, Pentecostals, Roman Catholics, Democrats, and Republicans, all sharing an imperial ambition.

The list of "Associates" belonging to The Family runs deep into our past and present national leaders. It includes Senators, Congressmen, Cabinet Secretaries, Supreme Court Justices, military leaders, CEOs, and the list goes on. Sharlet's book names names. To arouse your concern, consider this sample of names: Inhofe, Grassley, Domenici, DeMint, Brownback, Coburn, Thune, Pryor, Thurmond, Rehnquist, Thomas, Nickles, DeLay, Kemp, Baker, McCord, Magruder, Colson, Meese, Ashcroft.

The Family is convinced that being among God's chosen provides divine diplomatic immunity. The rules of man do not bind them, such as the separation of church and state, or the rules of the church, such as dogmas and morals.

This is an Elite Fundamentalism. It focuses on the up and out, not the down and out. It produces Key Men, selected by God, and clearly not based on their moral merit. God has chosen them as imperfect tools for God's own reasons, so don't judge them, because regular morals do not apply. They firmly believe that consequences do not apply to them because of the profound nature of the work that needs to be done, work they are chosen to do. Work that is not theirs but God's as told by Jesus. They are merely obedient. It's Jesus plus nothing.

Remember how at some point in the last seventy years, we added the words "under God" to the Pledge of Allegiance, and "In God We Trust" to our currency? Both those initiatives were driven by members of The Family. Sharlet's book describes the nexus.

The family has layers of unacknowledged leadership. Some are core members. Some host or attend Family-based prayer cells, some of which are held in rooms at the Pentagon, the Department of Defense, and House and Senate office buildings. Some of these folks participate in junkets all around the world to establish power relationships, spreading the message of Jesus plus nothing. Some have played important roles in establishing experimental laws such as the extreme anti-gay laws enacted in Uganda in recent years, and sexual abstinence programs across Africa.

Some of these folks, including Senators and Congressmen, live together in large houses in the D.C. area owned or managed by The Family. At least one of the homes enjoys tax exemption as a church. In these homes they sometimes entertain foreign dignitaries, eager to get in the good grace of The Family, from which many blessings flow.

The Family believes the powerful are the powerful because God chose them to be. Therefore, the reasoning goes, it is wise to get close to them, work with them, talk about Jesus with them, make deals with them. Do everything but judge them.

The Family desires power, worldly power, to build Christ's Kingdom cell by cell. One of the rare public ways in which they approach this work is through the National Prayer Breakfast. This highly covered full-house event, now shown on C-Span, owes its origins to The Family. They started it in 1953 and every President since Eisenhower has attended. It looks on the surface like a relatively simple couple of hours, one day a year, when national political and religious leaders convene for non-denominational fellowship.

But what we see on C-Span is just the icing on the cake. This is a multi-day event where power brokers meet and make deals. International leaders who are courting The Family or being courted come to D.C. to meet with politicians and corporate leaders. In meetings often brokered by The Family, they explore how they can continue to create a worldwide City upon a Hill through Biblical Capitalism, free-market fundamentalism, and imperial ambition. This is what they call Spiritual War.

Those at the core of this elite fundamentalism plant the seeds later nourished by those in the realm of popular fundamentalism. It was in this way that the Christian Right largely took over the Republican Party in the model The Family has for the world.

This co-opting led in significant measure to the transformation of the Republican Party from a generically conservative party to an increasingly rightist Christian party with a heavy emphasis on anti-gay, anti-abortion, free market, world leading, theology based positions. A particularly poignant example being "faith-based initiatives" spreading through state and federal agencies and programs. Faith-based initiatives are the intentional creation of The Family, intended to inch us closer to a theocracy.

These faith-based initiatives open the door for religious groups to the treasure house of social funding, along with an official stamp of government approval. The intense push for charter and voucher schools stands out as a particularly glaring and successful example. One wonders about their fingerprints on international charitable organizations.

It is easy for me to raise the suspicion that this sophisticated shadowy group lurks behind any given initiative, domestic or international, which seems to feed theocratic designs. But because they quietly play the long ball, it's very hard to know what they stir from behind, or how deeply behind.

In a mobius strip of manipulation, both Republicans and Democrats can be subtly coaxed into supporting some of grandest and most insidious elements of this theocratic agenda. Think of positive sounding ideas such as family values, faith-based initiatives at home and abroad, American exceptionalism, biblical capitalism, and the less benign-sounding, but all too often bi-partisan drift toward oligarchy. Perhaps this is what prompted Julius Nyerere, President of Tanzania, to declare, "The United States is also a one-party state. But with typical American extravagance they have two of them."

B esides considering and countering the manipulative effect this large cult is having on our civil democratic society, it remains imperative that we look at the implications beyond our borders. For instance, it would be terribly naïve to assume that other religious power interests (e.g., at this particular moment ISIS) in this world are not well aware of, even motivated by, much of what Sharlet's book divulges.

When you think about what The Family's brazen and clandestine purpose is, one begins to understand why much of the non-Christian world finds the U.S. not just perplexing but repulsive.

Good people from around the world find The Family's plot conniving, sinister, and insulting.

While her innocent citizens sleep...

CHEWING ON YOUR FATE

The **lounge car** on the Amtrak train has various seating arrangements. There are groups of two seats together. There are single seats alone, and there are combo sets of both, which angle toward each other – and a mirror image on the other side of a central aisle.

I'm taking up one seat of a two seat next to a single in a combo, waiting for someone. Up comes an extra large lady with her fat, adolescent son and asks me if I would move. She didn't say why the two available seats in my group of three would not be enough. They both leveled their gaze at me for a couple seconds, then looked away with an attitude that said, "Our readily apparent size should speak for itself." It was clear such a strategy had worked for them before. Something in our shared theatrical moment of playing on my sympathies, mixed with unspoken fatalism, struck me as pathetic.

But it worked. Without saying a word I picked up my book and my whiskey. With a wry smile, I simply moved to another seat across the aisle.

Curious, I watched over the top of my book (which was on the subject of chi) to see what they would do after their practiced, little theatrical victory. Sure enough, as soon as they lowered themselves, the mother unpacked her large bulging carry bag. She lifted out a big, plastic bag of gummy bears. Not a store bought bag, but a larger, heftier bag with a wire bag tie. This was a bulk deal packaged at home. The bag was big enough that once opened either of them could reach in their pudgy hand, grab a fistful, and still extract the bulging hand from the bag. They did this over and over. Mom, holding the bag, taking a handful. Next handing the open bag over to fat junior who did the same. They chewed and passed the bag back and forth for some time. To their credit, I thought, Mom eventually tied up the bag and put it back in her larger carry bag. Good, I thought, at least a modicum of discipline.

Mom didn't bring out an empty hand from the carry bag.

Instead, she held another home-packed, clear plastic bag; this one full of giant Sweet Tarts – multi-colored pastel discs, maybe a few hundred. Again, she undid the tie and they took turns grabbing a small handful and chewing them up, over and over. Mom eventually tied up the unfinished bag and put it back into the carry bag only to pull out her hand grasping a big bag of potato chips.

As I watched the porcine mother interacting with her bulging son, my female companion, who had come in about the time I moved, whispered, "That kid is doomed."

I'm overweight and riddled with imperfections. This isn't about weight. But the gluttonous consumption of factory food overloaded with salt, sugar, and other empty calories presents an unfolding tragedy to behold, and I just said so.

Amtrak brings us our own epic stories, both out the window and across the aisle. We turned our attention to the parade of countryside outside the window. Then a low, long, rumbling noise sounded from across the aisle. We both stood quickly and moved for the door, grateful the sound preceded the rest of the fart.

POSTCARD FROM THE NEW DELHI NIGHT

One thin candle warped by the heat of day now burns in the heat of night by a grass mat on an open, flat rooftop in a New Delhi neighborhood. We can't see the local night watchman, but listen to his stick strike the street with reassurance. The concrete street radiates heat... as does the rooftop which now hosts a trail of ants, apparently roused by the little candle flame in the heavy, still air. About midnight now and finally becoming cool enough to sleep till sunrise. But then, once the sun peaks over the roof lines and falls on our mat, it will within minutes be too hot to sleep. Paid twelve cents for a simple shave yesterday, only costs a nickel in the country. But we've left the country and are preparing to fly to Bangkok, unless the evidence we're set to see on Saturday confirms our friend's assertion there are exceptional carpet buys way up about three and a half miles from the Tibetan border. It must be daylight where you are, hope you enjoy today as much as we already did. A family sleeps on this roof with us; thousands sleep in the street, some by choice. In the family's courtyard below a fat dog sprawls in the dim shadows. In the distance an occasional scooter rickshaw purrs through the dark. Downstairs they will begin to make the first of many morning cups of tea about five a.m., before the heat of light comes and before the servant boy Ram arises. On the other side of this card Krishna smiles, impervious to heat and cold, day and night.

Taking a Bath on Chena Pump Road

In the summer of '69 I found an old log cabin for rent on Chena Pump Road, a few miles outside of Fairbanks, Alaska. This fine old cabin contained everything I needed, and everything I wanted except running water. I had an old pickup truck and a bunch of five-gallon containers. I hauled enough water to wash the dishes and my face. Everything worked well except for getting myself clean.

I put in overtime hours working on a survey crew in the long, warm, sunny days. I was doing alright, making good money, on my own, near the end of my teens; taking care of myself. I had a good place to live and a truck that ran. Only thing bugging me, other than a lack of love life, was getting clean.

I used to head up to the University some days after work and sort of sneak into a men's locker room for a shower, but that practice always came with the fear of getting caught.

One day I heard about someone giving away a big, old bathtub. White enamel coating on a heavy, iron, claw-foot tub. With a little help from my friends we got that beast of a tub into my truck bed and unloaded it in the secluded front yard of my cabin. We set the claw feet on concrete blocks. Now I'd be living in style. Couldn't wait for the weekend.

Friday evening I drove home with my half dozen five-gallon water containers full. Saturday morning I dug a little pit under the center of the tub and after filling the bath with water, built a fire.

I stoked the fire for hours as I went about my weekend chores, sticking my hand in the water to test the slowly rising temperature. It was a warm, sunny day, the hardwood fire crackled and smelled good, and finally the water started getting close to the perfect temperature. A couple more logs, a little patience, and my wonderful bathtub full of hot water looked really good. Just like mama used to fix for me.

So I stripped off my clothes in the afternoon sunshine of my secluded country yard and quickly jumped into the big tub, then even more quickly out the other side. It had not occurred to me the cast iron on the bottom of the tub was red hot.

Sometimes traversing the learning curves on the road of life can give you blisters on the bottoms of your feet.

Portraits in a Proper Parlor

Proper old school boarding houses still exist in some cities around the world. In old neighborhoods you still may find an aristocratic one, sitting there, rather stately, perhaps a bit musty. A certain dusty plushness infuses the air in these anachronistic interiors, where the tenants, each in his or her own bubble, find refuge from the boogie of the streets.

Fate stuck out its trickster foot and tripped me into this one in Washington, D.C. on a Friday, to wait for Monday.

There were four of them in the sitting room not counting the news man on the tube. At first only one looked up and it remained unclear whether she smiled. I could ask her, but I don't think she'll know. The house feels safe and strict, not suited to my tastes, but I'm out of the rain with no need to complain.

The soft, short-haired lady on the flowered couch keeps her coat over her legs, and her purse and papers over her pussy. Without saying a word she lets you know she is full of abstract love and untouchable. She would prefer I only speak to her or about her after she is dead. And she does not want to talk about that.

The one from Europe (Dutch?) worries out loud just a bit about getting out of D.C. in this downpour. Hell, I worry about staying in D.C. on a sunny day. He has some goals or maybe just agendas that keep him graying, suited, serious, and poised in a most practiced way. He's going to do just fine and not embellish much about it.

The Mister of the proprietors is primarily circumspect with his nose up in the air, interspersed with moments of shooting from the hip – which he does without lowering his nose. He has up to the hour information on the politics of the planet. He lets his wife have half her strength and he strokes that half with quiet determination. His establishment, the boarding house, resides all tight and polite and has everything a guest with a mind like his could need. He appears to be a withdrawing, angrily nonviolent asshole, though I'm not sure about the withdrawn part.

The Missus proprietor is authoritative with strange men. Yet she offers a pleading kindness and moves comfortably (cinematically, so she suspects). She knows how to stay quasi-approachable and warm in any occasion and feels violated if made to blush. She stands mostly thin except for her intestines. One of the ways she stays warm is by loving things about her asshole husband that are not even there. She's a potential junkie. She is a *"potential"* junkie.

The proprietors and their boarders abide in kindness without intention to hurt or steal. They do very little damage, especially to the environment. From head to toe they are far more intriguing than our leaders across town. They probably had some good mind altering experiences when younger, but never got lost too far over the edge of familiarity and comfort − or if they did they sneaked back with no one noticing. I wonder if they did that in nanoseconds or if it took a decade or two. Probably a mixed bag given there are four of them.

Anyway, they don't truck with such matters anymore. They have cultivated information that I have not attended to. They are precise in their phraseology and expect the same. Phraseology being more important than attire, you do understand.

They have not said one cutting thing to me... or, I bet, even about me. I find it oddly polite of them, as they suggest in no uncertain body language that I find my place in this parlor forthwith and remain there (quite welcome) minding my phraseology and giving deference to the evening news.

FLOATERS

This story connects two elderly American women and old Chinese Taoist mystics. The catalysts for the story are floaters. In case you don't know, floaters are little spots that float across the retina of the eye. Sometimes they appear roundish, some look like little DNA strands. They arrive mostly unwanted and are more common among the elderly. They simply show up and drift across the eye, especially in bright light. But to a limited and uncertain degree, they can be directed...if you don't try too hard.

According to the Mayo Clinic, floaters may look like black or gray specks, strings or cobwebs that drift about when you move your eyes. They appear to dart away when you try to look at them. Technically, they are mostly caused by age-related changes that occur when the jelly-like substance inside your eyes becomes more liquid. Microscopic fibers within the liquid tend to clump and can cast tiny shadows on your retina, which appear to you as floaters. The most fun and enticing part of that description is how they "appear to dart away when you try to look at them directly."

Once upon a time not so long ago, my wife and I were staying with her mother Gen for a few days. Gen is a spry, inquisitive lady in her eighties. She and her next door neighbor Gerry share a fence that separates their adjacent patios. Gerry is similarly well-read and good-humored. These two women have done and seen and heard a lot in the course of their lives, and digested their experiences well. In the course of a day, the two dear friends often find each other at the fence in their comfortable clothes and share a natural moment.

On one such day I was idling in a corner of Gen's patio reading when the two ladies happened to meet at their common fence. I couldn't hear what they were saying, but I witnessed a remarkable sight. The ladies began rolling their eyes, tilting their heads and chuckling. One would gently swat the air and they would laugh. To my great surprise and delight, I discovered they were playing with floaters, and had done so many times as they talked at the fence in the bright light. They would attempt to make them do figure eights and laugh in the playfulness of the moment, the play-fulness of nature, the playfulness of life. Elders detached from any particular purpose, but fully engaged in being alive, simply and beautifully present.

It occurred to me that these ladies were experiencing life in that moment the same as the Taoist masters of old. It was the pure, playful, unencumbered joy which characterized the wisdom the old Taoists found and became famous for, immortalized in lore, depicted as unpretentious and aware, sharing a joke with the world – the dance of life simply beyond words – identical with these old ladies at their common fence.

"AMERICANS"

T raveling in the world, especially in the Americas, I sometimes get called on the carpet when I casually refer to people from the United States as "Americans." We (people from the USA) seem to have expropriated the term for ourselves, to the exclusion of those from other countries in the Americas.

One pragmatic reason for this evolution in terminology is simply because we don't have an obvious, natural sounding alternative. Other American countries do: Canadians, Mexicans, Guatemalans, Bolivians...Sometimes in Spanish we're called, " stadounidense." But that is seven syllables, and not in our own majority language. "Norte Americanos" fails for those same two reasons, plus it rudely and crudely subsumes Canadians. Even "North Americans" is too awkward and disses the Canadians.

The other reason we call ourselves Americans is because we claimed it for ourselves. You might say it is emblematic of our self-described "American exceptionalism."

True enough, people from other countries have in large measure adopted the term Americans to refer to us, for the reasons cited above. It is the common currency of nomenclature.

But our exclusivistic claim to the name comes with a persistent edge of negativity. The strong tinge of arrogance is implicit, especially because we are, in fact, so omnipresent and bullish.

Everyone around the world knows who they're talking about when they say the phrase "The Ugly American." It ain't the Canadians, the Mexicans, or the Peruvians. So, in a powerful sense, that ship has sailed.

When I talk to thoughtful people from other lands, once I raise the subject, their eyebrows tend to perk up. They usually acknowledge this is a smoldering subject, albeit one that feels impossible to remedy at this point. Frequently, I hear foreigners say our usurpation and exclusive usage of the identifier "American" contains within it an inference of our arrogance. Again, our self-described American exceptionalism.

The whole Western Hemisphere got the monicker America in a strange and accidental fashion from a feminized version of the first name of one of many male European explorers who set foot on a tiny fraction of this vast land. A fluke of history. His mother would be shocked.

I have an idea. It's a fine idea and all but certain to fail. Out of respect for our fellow Americans from all the diverse countries in the Americas, what if we called ourselves USians? From a pronunciation perspective, I'm not saying "usians," as in "we-ians." I'm saying "USians," as in "U.S.-ians." To make that clear I would write it "USians." Everyone is familiar with the name "U.S." so it isn't an unfamiliar sound, and it is handy and descriptive shorthand. Did I mention the element of respect?

At the very least I hope I can engender a skosh of self-awareness and humility as we introduce ourselves to the world afresh each day.

FEATHERED APES

Next time you hear someone dissing a crow, punch him in the nose. Ignorance deserves correction. And homocentric arrogance deserves a punch in the nose.

A young crow hatches out to monogamous parents and can spend up to five years with its parents and their extended family. The baby crow is born with blue eyes, and then they turn black. When the crow matures it mates for life and can live up to twenty years.

Crows groom each other and engage in something akin to a funeral when one dies. You can notice them come into a death site, stand silent for a few minutes and then fly off silently.

But they are not always silent as every human ignoramus should know. So far we've discerned 250 distinct crow calls, plus at least two dialects.

Crows use their brains and plan ahead, unlike some people. A crow will take a walnut in its beak and fly up to just the right height so when dropped to the street below it will crack open, yet not shatter. Furthermore, a crow can time the drop in sync with a red traffic light so it will have time to come down and get the walnut without some idiot in a car trying to run it over. I bet you don't have a more impressive technique for opening a walnut.

And if you are one of those jerks who treats crows poorly, don't think you're getting away with it. In addition to generating bad karma, you place yourself on the local crows' shit list. They have good facial recognition skills and don't quickly forget a bad actor. In fact, they'll likely warn the whole neighborhood (and not just the crows) when they see you coming. Your reputation spreads like stink.

But generally speaking crows take more interest in tools than fools. Only crows, elephants, and some primates will make a hook to use as a tool. Try doing that without a thumb. Speaking of tools, a crow will use a tool to get another tool which it will then use to get food. I know people who can't connect that many dots.

Since crows abound on every continent, you can find an opportunity no matter where you live to pay some attention to them, show some respect, maybe learn something.

Now you should know enough so the next time you see someone harassing crows you'll have all the confidence you need to punch the ignoramus in the nose! The crows will be watching.

You can learn more about these fine feathered friends in a book by one of their friends, Lyanda Lynn Haupt. She calls the book "Crow Planet."

COMPASSIONATE NARCISSISTS

Maybe you know a narcissist, maybe there is one in your mirror. Maybe some of your best friends fit the description. If so, I hope they all abide within the benign subspecies of compassionate narcissist. I say so because although pit run, garden variety narcissists get boring in a hurry, compassionate narcissists comprise a curious and intriguing lot.

These people contribute to good purposes, have genuine compassion, and actively work to improve themselves. Yes, they are self-absorbed, sanctimonious, and sensually aroused by their own expressions of compassion – both in thought and deed. But I find them uncommonly nice people. The ones I've known I'd characterize as unusually bright.

Maybe we are all narcissists to some degree. Even those with low self-esteem protect their self-image with myopic self-serving thoughts of incompetence and unworthiness. Self-loathing as a form of narcissism…hmmm.

Compassionate narcissists come across much like your other fine friends, except for something a bit nebulous. Maybe you are less likely to knock on their door unannounced, concerned they would find you rude, a bit miffed by any inconvenience, anything that takes them out of their zone. Maybe they'd rather call you a cab than help you start your dead car.

Compassionate narcissists exemplify decency, typically true believers in peace. I am not railing against them. I'm struggling to describe some odd characteristics, rarely discussed, because…. after all, is this a problem? Who am I to judge? And why bother? Because I find it a strange juxtaposition: compassion/narcissism. How do these characteristics dwell and get along in one person?

I tend to admire these folks, even enjoy their company. I just want them to ask themselves about it…about the juxtaposing dynamics. And please, don't ask me. I don't have a list of my friends like that, so don't ask me if you're on it. If you think you should ask me, then maybe you are, but I don't have a list. Sorry I brought it up. Excuse me while I go out and find a problem. But let me say on the way out the door, if you are too self-absorbed you probably don't have the capacity to absorb these observations, anyway, so don't worry about it. Just keep on keeping on, and giving to good purposes.

Let me add this: at some place pretty close to the surface, compassionate narcissists do not like disruptions to their harmonious plans. Speaking of the surface, they tend to dress in what one might call "casual perfect," and if disheveled, disheveled just so.

Let us consider characteristics. A compassionate narcissist thrives in a zone he or she carefully made and refined. A bit cocooned. A bit overprotective because they believe their zone is better than the rest of the world, and therein lies a key to what I'm talking about. They feel sorry for the world, compassionate, but they don't really want to step fully into it because they might get some of the world's bumblefuck on their shoes. Similarly, they don't want people from the rough and tumble world getting too much into their space and contaminating their zones with the ups and downs and smudgey detritus of the world.

Good people. Typically among the best when it comes to leaving a modest footprint. This may help distinguish them from their cousins the Egotisticals. They don't need applause, accolades, or an oversize anything…they have a mirror.

Although it appears out of character, one commonly finds compassionate narcissists involved in spiritual practices. Might seem almost counter-intuitive that they would involve themselves in something innately humbling. But good spiritual practice can put you in the zone of well-being, and make you feel good about being there. Plus they are caring, and have an evolved sense of the world's suffering. They know how good life can be – because they found it for themselves, and blew a bubble around it.

Okay, I'm done. I'm leaving. I'm leaving it at that. This cannot be a big deal. As someone once said, "Vanity is a drop that makes the bitter cup of life go down."

I'm going to stop picking on the compassionate narcissists and go out and get a problem – one that sticks to my shoes. There I go, talking about myself again.

Too Much Relativity

I like my relatives (which include my in-laws). Some of them I consider friends. I even get a kick out of weird uncles. I like to go see them where they live, and I like it even better when they come to our house. I can enjoy a few days with them on their turf, and a little longer on mine. I'll readily spend the time and money to go see them, and eagerly wine and dine them at home. By now you might anticipate the next paragraph starts with "however."

However, there comes a tipping point. It is like cresting a lovely mountain with an impressive, craggy peak. The smooth mountain trail of our enjoyable visit starts to narrow. Stones become dislodged and I start to stumble on them as they tumble into an abyss. The worst part is the stones are all coming loose in my well-intentioned mind. The scene hasn't changed, the protocols remain the same, and worst of all the behavior of the relatives doesn't change either. It's me.

For the most part, the characteristics of my relatives fall well within the range of normal and acceptable. The world is easily big enough for all of them. But the pragmatic, if not charming, quirks and habits start at some point to create a dysfunction in my mind, dislodging my compassion and precipitating a most disconcerting avalanche of intolerance and a somewhat surreal perception of life around me. Perhaps I am a compassionate narcissist.

All of a sudden I realize I can predict what will be said next, and the response to it, and who will make it. I say to myself, no, no, no it can't be like this, but sure enough, I know what will come next and a sense of ennui floods through me.

It wouldn't bug me so much, but it all feels so mundane. So terribly mundane.

At this present moment, I know the tipping point is reached and what began as a wholesome and welcome opportunity to reconnect with extended family has become a slide into perdition. I breathe Kafka and Sartre, sometimes Rod Serling. I feel it like gravity and find no exit from the fall.

There I stood, holding my own on the family tree, and all of a sudden I silently yearn to be gone. I don't want to chop down the tree, I only want to morph into a ripe pine cone and fall off. But I know what I must do. I must look and move around as if nothing has changed, as if I'm happy right here, just like when we got together a few days ago.

All of a sudden what looked like a group of relatives sitting around a room drinking coffee and sharing observations, becomes for me a performance challenge like acting onstage in a play. Predictability is killing me.

In such a moment, it quickly becomes critical for me to speak less, minimize eye contact, smile when looked at, nod up and down. Do not grimace or glare. Do not nod side to side. Give no indication to anyone that we are in a surreal play. All my skill must attend to this moment, because if one of those relatives glances over detecting my angst and asks me what's wrong, the result could change our family dynamics for the rest of my natural life... and quite possibly beyond.

There is nothing to do but ride it out to its scheduled conclusion, trying not to listen too closely. Trying to avoid anticipating what mundanity will occur next, avoiding the predictable while adrift in a sea of redundant platitudes. I sit amazed at how little of what is said warrants being said.

Mick Jagger once said he finds magic in repetition. But he was talking about rock 'n roll, not family reunions.

But then the reunion ends, and almost immediately I find breathing space. When I try to reconstruct the whole experience, it occurs to me all the interpretive dancing inside my head sprang from my half-sighted mind run amok. The visit ran its natural course. For some, these days fulfill the year. I can be glad it happened and glad it ended. In the end it was relatively survivable.

A Man is a Fine and Simple Thing

We have a core group of friends including something less than a dozen couples and about that many singles. We get together socially (whoever's around) somewhat irregularly, usually on a weekend for a potluck, a bonfire, a sauna, a biking or boating outing, maybe a little late night dancing for those who are tuned up.

It's a loose but valued group of affiliated souls with whom you can tease, cajole, and relax. It's the pool from which one draws help to move something heavy or go on a bit of an adventure.

One spring day one of the guys in the prime of life died in a car wreck leaving a widow and child and stunned friends. At the funeral a half dozen of us guys got together and determined to meet in a year to commemorate our lost friend.

We picked the weekend of May 5th – well into spring but before the summer visitors come to the far north, and we rented a house in the woods of the Upper Peninsula of Michigan, just a short half hour north of Hurley, Wisconsin.

As I packed to go it was clear we were correct about being ahead of the summer travelers, but we miscalculated a little on the arrival of spring. Two days earlier, it had snowed up there all morning, nighttime temps hovered in the 20's, and the weekend forecast called for cold and rain up north.

But we were committed to honoring our friend's memory and, being mostly busy guys (one of us flying in from the West Coast), bad weather would not deter us from our purpose. Up to this point, all the wives were very supportive and proud of our intent; well pleased they had such caring men who had planned hiking, cooking, bonfires and some sort of commemoration.

But the weather forecast gave them some concern. When we tossed the last bags in the car, just as we were getting ready to pull out, the ladies said they were worried we would be cold, and limited in what we could do up there.

As I closed the car door I said, "Your concern is well taken and much appreciated. In the event of persistent inclemency, we shall endeavor to remain warm and dry and of good spirits by seeking shelter and camaraderie in the strip clubs of Hurley." My timing was impeccable. As we pulled away, we noticed a significant change in the nuanced topography of those female foreheads.

We cooked and ate well and honored our friend's memory, and that's all I'm going to say.

The Migrating Molar and My Birthday

Hi Kids,

Thanks for asking how I spent my birthday. It all started a couple months ago with some pain around my upper left wisdom tooth. It went away, then it came back. This went on for a while until I felt compelled to go to the dentist. He said my upper left wisdom tooth was migrating. When I went north the tooth headed south. He said the only practical long-term solution was to pull it out, 'cuz once it starts traveling, there is no stopping it. Then he added I better get the companion wisdom tooth on the bottom pulled at the same time. Why? Because with its counterpart/mate/grinding partner gone, everything the lonesome molar could do has negative implications. I analogized to my marriage to your mother and told him he better kill that tooth, too. He said no, this is a big deal for which you need an oral surgeon.

The oral surgeon stood tall and Chinese. I told him I didn't want general anesthetic; just shoot me up with a local. So I had two teeth pulled one morning. Pretty interesting sound to hear your teeth ripped from your head. They sent me home with about a week's worth of Vicodin which put me in a funk. The opioid took the pain out of my mouth and spread it evenly over the rest of the universe. Every glass I saw looked at least half empty and leaking. Apparently I don't like narcotics. Coulda fooled me. Must be an age-related loss of capacity because I used to enjoy opium.

By then it was my birthday, and I had developed a dry socket on the bottom, in the hole left by the tooth which had not caused any problem in the first place. That took about a week or more to fix with medicated stuffings. By then it became clear I'd developed another problem, to wit: I can't open my mouth wide enough to eat a goddamn peanut butter sandwich. I made an appointment to see the Chinaman the next morning. However, that evening when I went to open the barn door to get some hay for the sheepe, I disrupted a hornets' nest and got immediately stung on my left cheek. In the morning the Chinaman said the sore condition ("It only hurts when you open your mouth, right?!") is a spasm of the jaw muscle that became stressed during the extraction surgery, or likely so, but hard to tell about the swelling cuz it's exacerbated by the swelling from the hornet sting. He told me to take lots of ibuprofen and apply hot compresses. Did I mention the zit that popped out on my 59 year-old cheek right where I put the hot cloth?

How are things with you?

love,

    Dad

WHEAT DOGS

f you ever buy a ticket for Plovdiv, Bulgaria, at the train station in Sofia, be sure to stock up on food and drink before you get to your departure platform. Vendors line the walls in the station, but there's nothing for sale on the platform or the train.

We went to one of the little shops in the Sofia train station and bought a couple of what we supposed were some kind of sausage wrapped in a dough, all tubular and shaped like a hot dog. It looked like a corn dog without the stick except encased in a wheat-based bread, making it for descriptive purposes a wheat dog with mystery meat. Or so we thought. They looked pretty greasy. If we got hungry enough, we'd bite into them.

Trains always show you the grimy backside of a city, but on this one we had a compartment with a big window all to ourselves, so we didn't mind the scenery. Leaving the city the view enlarged dramatically, transforming into an epic panoramic movie entitled Bulgaria On Parade. It felt that way, except the movie stood still and the audience rolled past it. As far as the eye could see was gorgeous, bucolic country.

We hoped to have this compartment to ourselves the whole trip to Plovdiv, but people got on and off at various stops. The compartment had six seats, three on either side facing each other. The seats numbered 31 through 36. The ticket lady wrote 35 and 36 on our ticket in blue ink. Krista said she enjoyed having the compartment all to ourselves. I told her I had an idea. I could fix it so no one else would come into our space.

She looked at me a little sideways and asked how. I pulled out my blue ink pen and said I could write on our ticket just above where the ticket lady wrote our seat numbers the numbers 31, 32, 33 and 34. If anyone tried to come in I could show them the ticket and say in a firm voice, "We bought them all. Americans! Americans!"

Krista gave me one of those looks that says I still love you, but I'm not sure I know you, so I put the pen back in my pocket.

We sat back, hoped for the best, and I decided to count the ubiquitous plastic bags which clutter and defile the countryside. I lost count at a bazillion and didn't feel like starting over. By that time I'd worked up an appetite and dug out a wheat dog.

If you've ever thought you were buying a Bulgarian train station wheat dog, you probably remember it and may have had the same experience. The shop featured trays stacked with these things. We had made a hurried and impulsive purchase. Yesterday I'd seen the variety of meats in the market. Very fatty looking ground meat, also tripe and organs and pretty much everything between the whiskers and the tail seemed available. So we felt a bit trepidatious as we took them out of the grease stained paper the vendor had wrapped them in.

I was expecting something unpleasant, especially since we couldn't heat them. But they didn't smell bad and empty stomachs prevailed. So I held one up, looked at it, took a bite, and what do you suppose? Turns out I must've pointed to the vegetarian wheat dog tray because these babies came stuffed with cheese. And not too bad when hunger calls.

However, this story did not end at all as I had expected when I started writing it on the rhythmic, clacking train as I stared at the greasy paper.

By now the train was slowing for the arrival in Plovdiv. Listen to that word. Plovdiv. Didn't sound promising to my midwestern sensibilities. In fact, I quietly speculated a jilted lover whose ex still lived there named it as he headed out of town.

But that was simply my tin Yankee ear, the way I'd heard it slouched across seats 31 and 32 with my feet on 34 and 35.

Plovdiv turned out to be an enticing, welcoming city. A healthy mixture of the old and the new, generously sharing the same space. And the food was delicious – once I'd swallowed my preconceptions.

Storytellers in Dylan's Tempest

In 2012 Bob Dylan released an album called "Tempest." The storyteller in each song, in addition to the subject matter they describe, offers an uncommonly candid litany of his own characteristics. A hefty sampling of what each storyteller says about himself includes the following:

He's accused of being a gambler and a pimp, but he denies it.

He starts his day at midnight.

He dies numerous deaths.

His heart is cheerful.

He has a date with a fairy queen.

He'll drag two-timing Slim's body through the mud.

He walks across the desert.

He's armed to the hilt.

A heavy stacked woman crowned his soul with grace.

He buried his head between her breasts.

He loves women.

He ain't seen his family in 20 years.

He's grinding his life out.

He's drenched in the light that shines from the sun.

He pays in blood, but not his own.

He's got something in his pocket that'll make your eyeballs swim.

He's got dogs that'll tear you limb from limb.

He's sworn to uphold the laws of God.

He has low cards but he's going to play.

He's been out and around with the rising men.

He ain't dead yet, his bell still rings.

He ain't afraid to make love to a bitch or a hag.

He'll drink his fill and sleep alone.

He's got a flat-chested junkie whore.

He keeps his fingers crossed like the early Roman kings.

He spends forty-five verses watching the Titanic go down.

There are ten songs. Hard to say how many voices. I didn't find an overarching theme, and there was no reason to expect one.

The Yellow Line is for Decoration

Driving and parking in the U.S., generally speaking, contains little of interest, and less spontaneity, or fun. We are so rule bound that driving becomes little more than a programmed routine.

Not only have we made a rule for nearly every act or eventuality, we proceed with a firm expectation the rule will be obeyed…and enforced. Our disproportionate experience of the phenomenon called 'road rage' stems from inviolate expectations of specifically prescribed behavior when driving or parking.

We pay handsomely for the efficiency of parking police. Their systematic (often computerized) methods are designed and intended to catch the slightest violation of time expiration or inching slightly beyond a precise line or area. Obey the rules or keep moving.

Speaking of moving, whereas you will be promptly ticketed for parking in a marginally errant manner, you can expect equally prompt and much more severe punishment for moving infractions. The rules of the road fill volumes, and they only continue to grow. Law enforcement personnel are not only standing by, they are setting traps. We don't even question their increasingly sophisticated tricks.

And here in the U.S. we pay even more handsomely for increased personnel, intimidating uniforms and equipment, even clandestine equipment. You can get a ticket issued by a camera these days, the circumstances entirely unwitnessed and irrelevant. The penalty is nonnegotiable, and the punishments cumulative and exponential. In the land of the free we take pride in all this, we demand it, we ask for further limitations. We even use our cell phones (while driving) to report other drivers committing traffic infractions – or as we like to call it, "breaking the law." What a country.

Yet in the vast less harnessed wilderness we refer to as "the Third World," people somehow also get around. Yes they have laws governing the rules of the road, and some pertaining to parking as well, in some parts of this Third World. But mostly they get along valuing something we deem archaic and unworkable. Something we abandoned long ago. Something actually considered dangerous as an applied standard.

What is this something? It is a principle, a principle in two interrelated parts, both of which can be simply stated. They are The Golden Rule and Common Sense. Under this principle, traffic laws are more like guidelines than strict delineations of criminal acts.

You're driving around looking for a place to park and you see a spot. Ask yourself: if I park here will it inconvenience anyone? Will it block someone in? Is it going to make it hard for someone with a disability to get by? If the answers are no, park here.

If I double park here, put my flashers on, and run into that store to pick up some medicine for my Grandma, will cars and trucks still be able to get around me? Good. This is sure going to make things easier and quicker... and Grandma will get her laxatives a lot sooner, too.

What about crossing the center line to avoid a pothole or a stone in the road? In the Third World they call it common sense. Here in the land of the free we call it grounds for a search of the vehicle. And if you point it out too clearly for the officer, then it becomes grounds for incarceration, possibly preceded by a full body cavity search.

One of my favorite driving experiences in the Third World occurs when driving on a straight stretch of highway going faster than the car or truck I am coming up on headed the same direction. Meanwhile, a car is coming toward you in the distance in the other lane. Both of the other drivers assess the situation and without significantly changing speed, pull over a little, near the edge of the pavement in their respective lanes. This creates a circumstance where you now have a three-lane road and you, without significantly changing speed, make use of this temporary third lane and pass the car ahead of you. You might not want to do this if it looks like all three of you will be exactly abreast at the same instant, but otherwise it's a nice collaborative experience without inconvenience. How can you tell if it is appropriate to do this? Use common sense, and employ the Golden Rule.

In the Third World such practices expedite travel, make good use of the available space, and contribute to fuel efficiency. But in the States such behavior is a violation that may well go beyond a regulatory violation and be considered a misdemeanor crime – for which one of the other drivers quickly reports you on his cell phone after he stops yelling and swerving onto the gravel shoulder. Oh, and you will now have a criminal record for "reckless driving" which will raise your insurance rates, cost you points, and pulsate in wait for a second offense.

In more congested urban areas of the "less developed" world, what should you do? Switch lanes when it appears prudent (common sense), use your horn only when necessary for safety (Golden Rule), drive in the oncoming lane or up on a curb a little when practicality suggests. Don't drive in too big a hurry and extend courtesies to others.

As my friend Saiad Dowd told me while driving through Casablanca, "Don't try to follow all the traffic rules, you'll only make things worse."

Aspects of Tribal Sovereignty
in the 21st Century

*This essay is based on a talk I gave at the Ho-Chunk Nation Safety
Summit in Wisconsin Dells, Wisconsin, on April 23, 2013.*

In my thirty years as an Indian rights attorney and tribal
judge I learned to pay attention to what Native leaders have to
say, and to rely on their depth of experience to inform my own
thinking. I will draw from some of those folks in what I say here
today.

First of all, we need to talk a little about what tribal sovereignty
is, and what the exercise of sovereignty, which is often called
jurisdiction, means. My dear friend Judge Dave Raasch from the
Stockbridge-Munsee Band of Mohicans, the first Chief Judge
of his tribal court, likes to remind tribal leaders to always ask
themselves, "Are we exercising this sovereignty and jurisdiction as
'power over' our land and people or as 'responsibility for' them?"
That's a good reality check at all levels of authority.

Recently I had a chance to listen to Professor Matthew Fletcher
talk about tribal sovereignty. Matthew is a member of the Grand
Traverse Band of Ottawa and Chippewa Indians, a law professor at
Michigan State University, Director of the Indian Law and Policy
Center, and manages a very current and informative website
called Turtle Talk. He talked about sovereignty as a combination
of capacity and accountability. He talked about how dynamic it is
and, referring to how the Chinese have the same word for 'crisis'
and 'opportunity' called it 'crisistunity.' He noted how tribal
officials are much more accountable to their people than state and
federal officials, but cautioned tribal leaders not to hide behind
claims of sovereign immunity (more on that later). Matthew
reminds us that experiential sovereignty is the right to make your
own mistakes, learn from them and keep on going.

It is important to acknowledge what tribal sovereignty can be
used for:

- The preservation of tribal languages
- The protection of tribal culture through protecting sacred sites and objects, Native spiritual practices and ceremonies
- Economic security through compacts and agreements with other governments
- Law and Order
- Other basic government services.

It is important also to acknowledge how tribal sovereignty can be and is being exerted in Indian Country in what might be considered gray areas or emerging and innovative areas:

- Cross-deputization with non-tribal law enforcement agencies
- Civil citations of non-Indians into tribal courts, and perhaps criminal jurisdiction over non-Indians, as well, in certain circumstances
- Same sex marriages
- Planned parenthood–type services with a cultural foundation such as those begun by Cecilia Fire Thunder at the Pine Ridge Reservation in South Dakota
- Changes to tribal membership criteria
- Open adoption laws and practices. (Some tribes, including the Ho-Chunk Nation prohibit the termination of parental rights as contrary to tribal culture.)
- The re-emergence of indigenous justice. Traditional peace-making and traditional courts are on the increase in Indian Country. (For more on this see the essay "Peacemaking" herein.)

Tribal courts, whether modeled after the Western system or more traditionally based, are the place where most Native people will feel the power and the action of tribal sovereignty in the 21st century. And tribal courts are growing. It is up to Tribal Councils, Executives, and tribal programs to see and support this emergence. Protecting and exercising sovereignty will occur in tribal courts more than in any other arenas.

The growing significance of tribal courts will require improving access to justice in those local systems. The training and employment of tribal court advocates, guardians-ad-litem for the children, the disabled and the elderly, public defenders, peace-makers and mediators is expanding. Through this healthy growth the tribal courts are working increasingly well for the people they serve.

A word about tribal-state agreements. Reaching and utilizing formal agreements with a state agency is not a loss or abdication of sovereignty. Rather it is an exercise of tribal sovereignty. For instance, a government-to-government agreement on law enforcement includes the cross-deputization of officers from each participating jurisdiction. The officers go through each other's training and certification processes, carry each other's citation books and cite individuals into the appropriate court. Individual bad actors have their cross-deputization card jerked, and the agreement lives on in the efficient practice of protecting public safety, which remains in everyone's interest. These agreements are working around the country between tribes and states or counties and there are many models to look at. Well crafted agreements always carefully address the issues of sovereign immunity. Neither step on your neighbor's toes nor squander your self-determining future.

Ironically we have seen in recent years there are ways to protect and respect tribal sovereignty through creative enactments of state laws. Here in Wisconsin we have several examples. The recent passage of the Wisconsin Indian Child Welfare Act provides more respect and protection for tribal interests than does the federal law upon which it is based. The so-called 'Teague Protocols' (tribal-state Agreements based on state case law) and the 'Discretionary Transfer Rule' (a state Supreme Court made rule) not only acknowledge tribal court jurisdiction, but provide processes and formulas for finding tribal court jurisdiction to be superior to state court jurisdiction in some cases.

In the thick of all these emerging trends of law and policy, tribes must of course be seriously and vigilantly on guard against getting co-opted. This perennial problem is not likely to diminish in the 21st century. My dear friend and mentor, the late Reuben Snake of the Winnebago Tribe of Nebraska, used to remind people that to an Indian the "Melting Pot Theory" means 'we melt in your pot.'

Native legal rights are uniquely based on treaties, sovereignty, and land, and thus are different from those of any other race or ethnicity in America. The U.S. pushes toward a homogeneity that often is not in Indian Country's best interests. Sometimes the threat is inadvertent, sometimes it has been mean-spirited and intentional. Either way that trend poses a constant threat to Native rights and cultures.

If cutting a deal with a non-Indian entity requires too much compromise of who you are, don't do it. If accessing pots of federal or state funds means giving up too much of who you are and where you want to go, don't do it. I say so understanding how easy it is for me to speak it compared to how hard it is for you on the ground – on your ground.

One other aspect of protecting tribal cultures in the 21st century is something not much discussed. Indigenous societies, including Native American tribes in the U.S., are generally living more simply and closer to the earth than the majoritarian societies around them. Some of this comes from cultural choices, and some from the impacts of poverty. But the effect is an ability to survive on less. To live a little closer to the earth. Following that observation consider this: for reasons we are all aware of, the 21st century holds the foreboding possibility of a major societal collapse, whether from climate change, cyber war, economic collapse, and/or other causes. Meanwhile Americans, especially perhaps white Americans, are the most spoiled people in the world. They have become the most dependent on modern comforts and conveniences and the most inexperienced at basics – such as making a fire to purify water and stay warm, for instance. Consider this: If the internet goes out, we're back to 1979. If the electricity goes out, we're back to 1879!

Therefore, if a major societal collapse occurs, the U.S. will be the most dangerous place to be in the world. But Indian reservations will be much less dangerous, less chaotic, as will places like Mexico where people are still by and large more in touch with the earth in a somewhat sustainable way. So, I know this might sound strange, but your ability to get by on your land on the margins of society may save you from a truly awful fate.

Speaking of the importance of having your own land, I would like to share a story that really brings the point home. Right on the cusp of the Millennium, in December of 1999, I had the good fortune of traveling to Cape Town, South Africa, with eight Native American spiritual and political leaders to participate in the Parliament of the World's Religions. This was occurring at a time when South Africa was in the process of rewriting their post-apartheid Constitution. Somehow, a number of South African tribal leaders and elders learned that the delegation of tribal leaders from the U.S. was going to be there and they journeyed down to Cape Town and requested a meeting with their U.S. tribal counterparts to discuss an important question. It was an unexpected development. Schedules were changed, an entire afternoon was set aside, a very large table was set up in a hotel conference room, and about twenty tribal leaders from the two countries, along with interpreters, took a seat for an unprecedented moment in time.

The question posed by the South African tribal leaders was essentially this: We are aware that after the non-indigenous invaders came to your country there was a painful process that included the drafting of the U.S. Constitution and the struggle of tribal people and cultures to survive in the implementation of that Constitution for the past two hundred years. We here in South Africa are at the same moment where such a Constitution is being drafted for the future. What do you think are the most important things for us to protect and insist on in our Constitution in order to ensure our sovereignty and the survival of our tribal cultures in this larger society?

It was an incredible afternoon. As the opportunity to speak went around the room, the answer from the U.S. tribal people to the question posed by the South African tribal people was unanimous. The answer was "land." Next on the list were culture and languages.

There is another somewhat sensitive subject which belongs in a discussion on protecting tribal sovereignty in the 21st century, and I'll phrase it this way: "Watch out for Conservatives and Liberals." Just in passing on this topic, I'd like to say one more thing I learned from Reuben Snake, and recently heard similarly from Sherman Alexie. Indian people tend to be politically liberal, and yet more conservative in their personal values. I'll leave that right there and let Native people sort it out for themselves.

My point is that both conservatives and liberals pose threats to Native sovereignty. Let's take the conservatives first because that's the easiest, the low hanging fruit. While Americans in general push toward homogeneity nationwide (for instance less regional in food, speech, architecture) the conservatives are less sensitive and accommodating toward Native interests impacted by that trend.

More insidious is the creepy response to what demographers and ethnographers are calling the "browning" of America, but which the redoubtably ironic Reuben Snake more correctly called the "re-browning" of America. It is essentially that in the coming decades we will see people of color become the majority of Americans. It has created a very quiet and subterranean response in certain circles which can be described as the consolidation of the white Christian power structure. Think tanks and legislators are talking confidentially about it, considering strategies, doing what they can without being grossly overt.

In my opinion, the most powerful and influential place where this is occurring is the U.S. Supreme Court. I will cite briefly three examples. The first is the peyote case where the Court said one of the oldest religions in this hemisphere, practiced by Indians, would no longer be protected by the Constitution's Bill of Rights guarantee of Free Exercise of Religion. Justice Scalia, in writing for the majority, said that interpreting the Constitution's Free Exercise of Religion clause in such a way as to protect this particular Indian religion is "a luxury our democracy can no longer afford." He went on to say if Indians want protection for their religion they should go to Congress. He said this knowing the Bill of Rights was enacted specifically to protect individuals and minorities from the "tyranny of the majority" in Congress.

The second case I'll cite is the more renown case called "Citizens United" which opened the floodgates for those with money to influence law and policy. The third case is another Indian case, the Lara case, where Justice Thomas wrote that tribes no longer have sovereignty since the end of the treaty era. I cannot understand what he means and, thankfully, the majority of the Court (although ruling against Indian rights) did not buy into such a scary argument. But because it could even be put on paper in a U.S. Supreme Court opinion in the 21st century, it is very troublesome.

I'll drop this topic here because I'm not a conspiracy nut, and what I'm citing is amorphous, perhaps unprovable. But if I can look at the demographics and think of the consolidation of the white power structure, so, too, can those who control that power structure.

Turning to the liberals, the dangers come from a different direction. Yes, I think it is true that generally speaking conservatives are more likely to be antagonistic to tribal interests, but liberals can create risks in the guise of support. Liberals often unintentionally undermine tribal rights. For instance, I don't know how many times over the years I've been in conversations with liberal friends about the Indian Child Welfare Act and the rights of tribes to re-interpret what non-Native social workers and courts call the "best interests of the child." Liberals will often say, "Wait a minute. We're talking about children here. Tribal rights have to take a back seat to that." Liberals take such a view not to eviscerate tribal rights, but without realizing the tribe's interests in the child are part of the child's best interests.

Another area fraught with messy implications that threaten the integrity of Indian culture has to do with the co-opting exploitation of cultural and spiritual practices. Here are a few examples:

- Non-Native anthropologists wanting to dig up Indian graves so they can study and understand Indians... respectfully, of course, and for the Indians own benefit – as the anthropologists are quick to insist. Ever try to dig up a white guy so you can understand them better?
- Non-Natives suing for the right to have eagle feathers so they can practice their "Indian-related" religions. This despite the already too few eagle feathers available through the national repository to meet the ongoing legitimate needs of Indian people. And taking the matter to unsympathetic non-Indian courts creates a further risk of curtailing Native rights. "Either I get eagle feathers too, Your Honor, or the Indians have to give up theirs."
- Non-Natives expropriating peyote and the ceremonies of the Native American Church, creating further legal risks for the real church members, creating shortages of peyote for real church use, and generally insulting the integrity of the religion with sacrilegious embellishments.
- Non-Natives insisting on the right to not only participate in, but control, sweat lodges in prisons. Their disruptive, disrespectful behavior has resulted in prisons canceling the practice of sweats entirely.

The 21st century, like every other century, will be a critical time for indigenous cultures here and worldwide. The pressures for uniformity and homogeneity are intense and getting worse. At the same time tribes in the U.S., Canada, and elsewhere, are finding their footing after the brutal devastations of the conquest era. The value of indigenous thinking, of Indian ways, is becoming more seriously recognized and appreciated just as the majoritarian systems and world views are losing their previously unquestioned cachét.

Despite the resurgence of Indian cultures, the pressures against them never go away. I conclude with a story of an evening I will never forget because it informed my entire career.

I was at a Tribal Council meeting on the Winnebago Indian Reservation in Nebraska in the mid '80s. As the Tribal Council was meeting late into the evening on some pressing matters, in walked Browning Pipestem. Browning was Oteo-Missouria/Osage, a prominent Indian attorney and an imposing and colorful character. He was given the floor and reported that he was just then returning from Washington, D.C. where a federal agency had done something really stupid which would impose additional hardships on tribes and threaten their powers of self-determination.

Norma Stealer, a strong Winnebago woman on the Tribal Council, put her hands on the table and said in exasperation, "Browning, when does this end?" Browning stood to his full height and said, "It ends when you give up."

JUST BECAUSE

Just because I might count my steps walking in the woods or count them up to sixteen and then start over. Or just because I move my finger underneath my pillow so I can hear it as I lay in bed. Or just because I keep a beat with my fingers or my whole hand when driving even when the radio is off. Just because I buy a year's worth of my favorite unscented soap at a time in case they quit making it. Or just because I pretty much know where all my books are. Or just because I can imagine a little rhythmic song that goes in and out with my breath. Just because I go to elaborate lengths trying to keep squirrels out of my birdfeeders. Or just because I build more fences or roofs around our place every time I think I might lose my job. Just because I leave my left shoe on the left and my right shoe on the right when I take them off. Just because I might occasionally play a little pocket pool. Or just because I refill my stapler as soon as it runs out. Or just because I keep my paper clips sorted by size. Just because I have about thirty extra bookmarkers all kept in the same place. Just because I trim my fingernails without tools. Or just because I try not to get a phrase of a song stuck in my head doesn't mean I'm OCDC. Doesn't mean I have Obsessive Compulsive Disorder Compulsively.

The Green Monster Off Its Leash:
Symptoms and Treatment

"Some people tell you the worryin' blues ain't bad

But it's the worst feeling, oh I ever had."

The Green Monster ranks as one of the oldest afflictions known to humankind. We find it described in the earliest writings of humans worldwide, and referenced throughout the world's religious and tragic literature. The technical name of this disease is Infidelity Mistrust and Anger Disorder (IMAD). There are a variety of colloquial names, such as "the worryin' blues" or "mental malaria," found in certain artistic circles and neighborhoods. IMAD is a debilitating, neurotic disease, similar in many respects to malaria. Excruciatingly painful, it is systemic, affecting primarily the heart and mind, but abiding in one's bone marrow. Although the initial onslaught is often the most severe and painful, it is common to experience a relapse.

The duration of a remission tends to increase unless conditions favorable to its recurrence are manifest. Conditions that can trigger a relapse include but are not limited to the following: fatigue, melancholy, a random quip, an absence, a phone call where the caller hangs up when you answer, stubborn selfishness, unrequited love.

Factors known to send the Green Monster into remission include sex, simple reassurance, assorted intimacies, a double dose of empathetic love, clear expressions of truth. It is important to note that if the object of the jealousy and mistrust withholds available treatment, he or she may be subject to emotional bruising and/or separation. Permanent scarring may result. It may even prove contagious.

The only long-range treatments for which there is empirical evidence of a cure are Time and Love. Time, in addition to being the wisest counselor, is a portable sanitarium for the treatment of

IMAD. Love, in significant and perpetual dosage, has proven to be the most effective prescriptive antidote.

In the case of an eruptive relapse when neither Time nor Love are available antidotes, there is some anecdotal evidence indicating that if the patient has access to a ready supply of tiki torches planted so nicely along the shore, temporary relief from the most debilitating symptoms may be effectuated by emphatically smashing the tiki torches to smithereens. However, caution must be used in such circumstances to guard against unpleasant side effects, most notably fire and police.

LET US EXAMINE MYTHS

Myths get a bad rap in our modern western world. Both religious and practical people often portray myths as messy and superfluous, nuisances, in the way of our utilitarian goals. Like flowers gumming up the machinery of modernity. Too many of us do not think myths have a place in our sophisticated lives.

Not so fast there, Mr. Businessman. Let's take a look under the hood, starting with a simple little verse.

> *The sun is up*
> *it's ten o'clock*
> *we're heading north*
> *across the border*
> *it's quiet there*
> *in the month of May*

None of the lines in this little verse is true. For instance the sun is not up, it is not going anywhere, it is already here no matter where we are in relation to it – as we twirl around on an orbiting planet. What does "up" mean?

And it is not really ten o'clock. That's just a smart myth we concocted to help us measure things that exist near and far in time.

There is no such thing as north. Try looking for it on the moon. North is simply a magnetic-based myth we use to find our way.

The earth does not have borders. You only have to ask the birds or the wind for a simple confirmation of the obvious. Borders are man-made, imaginary lines configured with fences and gates... and sometimes guns.

Quiet is such a relative concept. A deer or a dog or a sensitive audio machine will not agree about quiet here or there or anywhere.

Nature knows no month of May. The earth turns with repeating regularity, but no natural moment occurs when something called April ceases to exist and all of a sudden May appears like a solid rock.

These myths, these constructs, these concepts, have no independent existence. They only have the reality we as humans give them. Yet these and other myths serve as the man-made foundations upon which we create our societies and civilizations.

So let us be careful, be mindful as we in these modern times tend to use the word myth dismissively, nay even as a pejorative. For the power of myths makes our world go round, even the metaphor itself a myth lending meaning. Those basic myths shape our understanding even before we begin talking about the great archetypes and classic stories – the myths that feed our souls.

Stuck Here Now

First trip to a nation one feels a bit obliged to pay some dues, make the rounds of some of the respected sites for which the people and places earned a reputation and now polish their pride. It can easily feel like you move around too much, too much schlepping, don't really take the time to get acquainted.

So while we're making our way through famous venues and the well-worn paths between them, I'm casting a curious eye toward the local and obscure. All the while my wife and my conscience remind me to pay attention to the history and ambiance that surround me. Get your head in the present, the theory goes, and enjoy where you are on this famous path. Take it in, soak it up. This is it. Be where you are. So I let go of my idyllic, little longings and try to adapt best I can the old Ram Das adage and figure it's alright. I'm stuck here now.

Once you've resigned yourself, I mean, embraced where you are and get used to that good, stuck-here-now feeling going on, you still face the vexing giant question of technique. How to be where you are. The micro version of the macro problem we just discussed. The question turns out to be a dialectic that has been ongoing among travelers forever. Some people are eager to get out there and explore every nook and cranny and leave no picturesque cobblestone street untraversed, no hilltop unconquered, no religious edifice unbreached, and certainly no recommended traditional anything unvisited. My wife is among them. Others of us, not so much.

The issue is not that I don't have curiosity and interest in other cultures; it's a question of technique for experiencing them. I arrive more than willing, often eager, to position myself in the stream of some new part of the world. Now to the problem. Instead of rushing around in search of the nuanced hearts of the country, I prefer anymore to position myself in just a few select places. El Centro or some zocalo is usually a good bet. Let the country pass by me at its own rhythm and pace.

Metaphorically, I am the standing wave in a good feng shui spot of a river of foreign culture, and whatever that river consists of flows right around and through me – rather than being a surface wave that keeps rolling along until it crashes up on a shore. (You can't beat a good metaphor that demonstrates your point and leaves the opposition foundering on the rocks.)

Some people I know prefer a decidedly different technique. I won't mention names, but I am talking about my wife. While I begin to relax with a local drink in a sidewalk café, certain people are compelled up every colorful cobblestone calle. Next thing you know some classic traditional-looking old lady invites her into her shop or home "just look, no problem." We are now past the point of returning empty handed. Maybe she returns with the shawl right off the old lady's back. These sweet old ladies are something else; specifically, kind and crafty entrepreneurs.

It doesn't cost much to sit and drink, maybe converse with the locals (who aren't selling anything). Additionally, you don't have the growing problem of more to schlep, which can easily result in more shopping for another bag to put it in. Have to support your local craftsmen, she says. Well, vintners are craftsmen, too.

It is not, of course, an either/or proposition. It is simply a matter of proclivities when it comes to choosing ways of experiencing a culture. For instance, a couple of days after the last old-lady-hawking-shawls-in-Crete event, I was lingering over a coffee in a hotel lobby in Sofia. Others rushed off with circled city maps. There in the lobby I learned the Bulgarian aphorism that goes, 'No man is bigger than bread.' The fellow told me it was very important to understanding the Bulgarian psyche and I suspect he's right. In hard times you look to the basics.

On the other hand, had I not joined my wife for a trip to the Ethnographic Museum, I wouldn't have learned another Bulgarian axiom, 'Not all good is for good.' I took it to mean beware of conniving leaders.

This is probably a cheap shot, but I'll note the first aphorism came with a free cup of coffee, whereas the other required a long walk and the price of admission.

INFORMING AS A LIVELIHOOD

You want to know what scares me? I'll tell you, but first a little background. In the United States we are experiencing a dramatic demographic drifting apart of the haves and the have nots. This pernicious, slow motion trend affects the dynamics of our culture... and not in a good way. The number of citizens feeling disenfranchised grows. It includes the unemployed, the under employed, those working two or more low paying jobs, those who have given up, and those with steady jobs whose stagnant pay does not keep up with the cost of living.

The haves are rolling along in the American dream. The have nots are losing ground. They need food, clothing, decent shelter, a bigger piece of the pie, and, of critical importance, a sense of self-worth.

Neither the Congress nor the President nor the voting public has the balls to create a contemporary version of the Civilian Conservation Corps or the Works Progress Administration. They're looking for an easier way to get a lousy fix, kick the can of collapse down the broken highway. And make some money at it. And they have no shame. How can they diminish the risk of unrest, keep order and pride in America, throw a bone to those in need, and hopefully realize a net profit to the government coffers?

Now we get to the part that scares me. What does any typical government do when they feel the threat of unrest and disruption to the status quo? Do they embrace innovative change? Hell no. They double-down on enforcement of law and order.

And what better way to do that than to get the good citizens to do it for you — with good morals and public interest on their side. And yes, it will be said, at least implicitly, that God is on their side, also.

It might start in one of the states. One with just the right political chemistry and maybe some shocking exposés of moral and criminal misbehavior of a sort I'll get to in a minute. But this is the U.S.A., so it could start as a federal program if enough pundits and commentators can see to it there's enough blood in the water to start a feeding frenzy for 'reform.' Perhaps it begins as a pilot project, fed by fear, to stop the outrage and restore dignity to the honest working man or woman by reasserting pride in the nation so many have fought and died for... or some bullshit like that. But whether it starts with a state or a federal program it will spread throughout the state and federal systems through a process both messy and opposed, but in the end will succeed because the easily duped voting public will insist on it.

Here is the loathsome idea. We are going to pay people to inform on each other, turn each other in to the authorities for committing crimes and violations. I'm not talking about the typical undercover cop or the sleazy snitch trying to keep his ass out of a sling. I am talking about the common man in an overt, above board, publicly supported program of enforcement of moral and legal standards we all believe in, blah, blah, blah. Some folks might form organizations to do this work. But probably for most the design is freelance.

You know somebody who subverted some cash to avoid paying taxes on part of their income? Some farmer selling raw milk? Somebody using plant seeds in contravention of Monsanto's copyrighted GMO's? Somebody committing acts of pollution or disconnecting the pollution control device on their truck. (You have to have the Democrats on board, you know.) You know somebody using drugs? Hunting out of season?

There will be fee schedules for reporting illicit acts to the proper authorities. Some big ticket items will pay not just a flat fee but a percentage of the government's take beyond a base amount. The argument will be about those amounts, not about the true, underlying, awful nature of the programs.

As you can see, there is nothing wrong with simple civilian participation in the enforcement of our cherished and highly evolved legal system. Our "American way" of life. Our standards. In fact, this patriotic insistence on toeing the line is not only in the public interest, but an innovative, entrepreneurial initiative, part of the fabric of our capitalist system...call it a civic duty. Keeping America safe. Try not to think of it as a bounty system.

The participants no longer feel idle or left out, the government takes its cut in penalties and back taxes as a revenue raiser without raising taxes, the public-minded informants make some money, their self-esteem rises... and they pay taxes on their income. Everybody plays by the rules. Bingo!

Why would any God-fearing, tax-paying, good citizen not support a program like this? All you have to do is make sure you always color inside the lines and you shouldn't have a problem.

PROSELYTIZERS

Of all the lowly and nefarious professions, proselytizing gripes me the most. No matter how you couch it, the essential message from proselytizers is this:

Everything you know is wrong. The core of life comes from the name I believe in, and all truths and values inexorably flow from that. Because my way is so superior, generous, and necessary, I have come here to share it with you. It is the final, religious truth, set in stone and blood. You can either join us and be among the fortunate who have the correct and comprehensive way of living life, and are guaranteed a saved and idyllic afterlife, or you can reject the truth. If you reject the truth, you will wander in ignorance and ignominy, and I am sorry to say, die miserably alone into eternal damnation. The choice is yours. Oh, and by the way, I love your hat. Your culture has so many lovely things in it. I just love it here. Do you have a few minutes to look at this little book with me?

Our Family Christmas Letter

Season's Greetings to all our friends.

Well, this has been another excellent year for the Botsford family, and we wanted to share all our news with our dear friends near and far. Tenzin received an appointment from the United Nations to serve as a Special Goodwill Ambassador to Central America. We were particularly pleased to have our dear friend Kofi Anan take time out of his busy schedule to come to our vast acreage to make the presentation in person. So Tenzin will be putting a trailer hitch on his Humvee and moving in an adventurous way to a townhouse in Houston so he can make quick forays to the countries he serves and still get home for the weekends. He is such a joy and we are so proud of his many accomplishments. Katelin was once again voted Most Popular Girl in her school, and this year we were so pleased she was also voted Most Likely to Succeed. These are honors she deserves and we continue to be so proud of her. Guess we'll have to add another trophy shelf again to hold all her awards. Speaking of awards, as you all know she's a senior this year and the competition by the colleges and universities to persuade her to attend was at times vicious. I'm sure you all agree after awhile it just gets tedious having all these college recruiters calling and coming around. (Though we do enjoy the free dinners and little enticements.) Katelin has pretty much made up her mind to go to a private school, although some of the public universities did make great offers with full scholarships and whatnot. Still, in the end, we thought it best and safest to send her to a private school, even though it will be more costly. Can't say which one it will be because several of them are still bidding for her, but we'll be sure to tell you all about it in next year's Christmas letter. Krista has toured and lectured in all her favorite counties, with her seminar presentations on Spinning and Weaving for Feminists. We had no idea how popular she would become. Sometimes we just wish the requests would quit coming in so quickly. She hardly has time to unpack and relax before she's off to another continent. Hiring a personal assistant for her has turned out to be a godsend; don't know how she got along without her. I guess it's just like getting your first nanny. At first you wonder if you can ever keep them busy (to say nothing of trusting them), but pretty soon they become almost indispensable for looking after all the mundane details of daily living, especially when you have such a big house with lots of outbuildings. Anyway, we did manage to get a bit of a well-deserved break this year. We were so fortunate to be able to spend six months in Tahiti with the kids and the pets. I don't know how we were so lucky to get Marlon Brando's villa for just the exact six months we wanted it. It was kind of embarrassing when we got the bill and realized that the staff at the villa was not included in the price. Of course, by that time we were back at home and it was too late to properly thank them and tip them. One just doesn't dare send money through the mail to a place like that. I'm sure we've all had those experiences. James continues to amaze us all with his renaissance abilities in so many fields. Words simply cannot describe his contributions to civil society. We were especially proud this year for his two well-received TED talks and matching book contracts. Love those advances. Keep 'em coming, James!

We sure enjoy your Xmas cards and photos. Such beautiful paintings and sweaters. They can do so much with acrylic these days.

XXOOXXOO

How We Upgraded Our Computer

When I came in the door my wife was on the phone. Krista asked the caller to hold and asked me if I would take the call because she was in the middle of something else. Krista said she couldn't vouch for the lady's legitimacy, but that she had called before saying it was on behalf of Customer Service at Microsoft.

I got on the phone, we introduced ourselves and the following conversation ensued:

ME: Now why is it you're calling?

SHE: I'm calling from Customer Service at Microsoft. You purchased some Microsoft programs several years ago, and it's our experience that those older programs lose some of their speed and versatility over time, especially if your computer is older and has been subject to viruses and is sluggish.

We value our customers, want to keep you, so I'm calling to suggest you take your computer to the Geek Squad at your local Best Buy, I can give you their number, or if you'd prefer, we could try to help you clean up the junk in your computer and upgrade it over the phone.

ME: Is this going to cost me something?

SHE: No, sir. It's a customer service. It's completely free of charge. Like I said, we value our customers and want to keep them.

ME: Are you trying to tell me you don't want me to switch over to Apple?

SHE: (Laughs) Well, sir, I'm not supposed to say it that way, but yes, we want you to continue to be satisfied with our products.

ME: And you're sure this isn't going to cost me anything? Because I hate phone solicitations.

SHE: No, there's no charge. Well if you take your computer to the Geek Squad there's probably some charge, but if you want to try do it with our help it is absolutely free. It's entirely up to you. Are you pretty well-versed in using your computer?

ME: No, I'm not. I'm a neo–Luddite. Our computer is old and sluggish. I've imposed on a friend to help us clean it up, but I hate to do that and some things no longer work very well.

SHE: Well, as I said, it's entirely up to you. You don't have to do anything, of course. But if you'd like I can give you the phone number for the Geek Squad at your local Best Buy, or, if you like, we could try to walk you through it.

ME: How do I even know who you are? Not to be rude, but you could be anybody.

SHE: Well, as I said, I'm from Microsoft. If you want to go on your computer I could pretty easily prove I'm from Microsoft.

ME: Okay, I'm on my computer.

SHE: Do you see an icon down in the corner? Click on that. Now click here (she described where), and here. Now, do you see the Windows logo on the screen followed by the words "Microsoft Support Service?" Now you can see that we really are in Microsoft Windows Support Services. If you click here (again describing), and then here, you can see the list of all the viruses that have infiltrated your programs causing the problems you're having. I can see your screen now too. Do you want to proceed?

ME: Well, maybe, but…

SHE: (A bit exasperated). I tell you what. I'm going to give you to my supervisor.

(Pause)

HE: Hi. This is Kevin Parker from Microsoft's Tech Support Team. Amy just told me your computer is a bit sluggish and some of our Microsoft programs aren't working as well as you wish they would, or as they used to. But that you're also looking for some assurance that we are who we say we are. Is that correct? It's very understandable, sir. How can I help?

ME: Well, I really just don't see any way to get to a comfort level about who you folks are.

HE: My job is to help. I love my job. This call is being recorded. I want to satisfy you. I don't want to lose my job. Do you see this thing I'm putting on your screen that has the Windows logo and says "Microsoft?" Only Microsoft can do this. Now do you see the icon and numbers at the bottom of the screen? Click on that. Okay now that I'm into your programs, let's look again at all those viruses and errors. I can bring them up. Now I'm going to just erase them all… scrolling down, there they go. Alright your system is all cleaned out, and it will work a lot faster now.

ME: Well, yes, it looked like they all got emptied out of my machine here.

HE: Would you be interested in buying a warranty from us that will protect you against this happening again and give you access to our assistance to keep your Microsoft programs clean and working well?

ME: I don't think so.

HE: This is a unique promotional offer. It's $10 for one year, or $15 for three years, or $20 for the life of the computer. All you have to do is click on which one you want on the screen I'm putting up there and enter your debit card number in the box at the bottom.

ME: I don't want to do that.

HE: Look, only dots will appear when you enter your number. Watch. I'll put my own in there, see? I won't even see your number. Just dots. Look, I wouldn't abuse this even if I could. I don't want to lose my job. Tell you what, do you have another phone, like a cell phone?

ME: Yes.

HE: I'll give you the number of our Team Leadership office in Seattle. I'll hold on this line, you call them on the other phone to verify that this is legitimate. My name is Kevin Parker, my employee number is ...... Call our main office to verify who I am and that this is a legitimate Microsoft Warranty promotional online offer. Here is their number.

ME: (After calling the other number.) Well, I called and heard a voice answer saying it was Microsoft, and heard the chatter of a phone bank in the background but somehow he couldn't hear me.

HE: Okay. We'll try again.

ME: (After calling again.) I did it. Same problem.

HE: Okay. I don't know why he couldn't hear you. Well, please just select which warranty you want and enter your debit card number. Don't give me your credit card number, and don't even enter the Pin number for the debit card.

ME: I'm just not comfortable doing that. Send me the bill by mail and I'll pay it.

HE: It's just $10. This is only an online offer.

ME: Sorry. I can't do that. But you already deleted the crap from my computer so I'm okay now, right?

HE: Yes, it's clean now. But you immediately become vulnerable again. Activating the warranty right now is the only way to guarantee keeping your system clean and protected.

ME: Okay, so just bill me.

HE: Look, type in your debit card number or your whole system could crash.

ME: Why would that be? You're starting to scare me.

HE: This is your last chance to give me the number.

ME: Well, I guess this proves you're not from Microsoft after all.

HE: This is truly your last chance. Type in your debit card number or I will destroy everything on your computer so completely that you might as well just throw it in the garbage can.

ME: Do you have any integrity?

HE: Very last chance.

ME: Can't do it. Please, what would you gain by destroying my files? It must be clear to you now that I'm not going to do it. Why don't you just back away and leave us alone without destroying what we have? You have nothing to gain by it.

HE: You wasted thirty minutes of my time. Watch your screen. See that? There it goes.

I watched helplessly as everything was erased from the screen, page after rapid page, until the screen went black. The computer was dead, would not restart.

I ate a heaping helping of humble pie and drove down to an electronics store where we bought a new Mac. The Geek Squad retrieved our most important files, and now they are behind icons up in the corner of the screen on our brand new virus-protected Mac. And that, unfortunately, is how we upgraded our computer.

NOT MEETING SANDRA DAY O'CONNOR

My wife and daughter did not know Sandra Day O'Connor and neither did I. As strong, contemporary women, however, they certainly knew of her and took some satisfaction that she was the first woman to serve on the U.S. Supreme Court – a significant and long overdue accomplishment.

I, on the other hand, knew more about her. In my thirty years as an Indian rights attorney I had watched her tenure on the Court and had participated in an amicus brief in one of the most important and devastating Indian rights cases in the latter Twentieth Century. I will tell you why we did not meet her at a roadside rest area in northern Wisconsin. First, a little about the case to explain why we didn't meet.

The case involved the rights of Native Americans to use peyote as a sacrament in the religious ceremonies of one of the old Native religions – called the Native American Church (NAC). The case got to the Court when a zealous program director fired a Native American drug counselor from his job in Oregon for attending peyote ceremonies of the NAC one Saturday night in the 1980's. This 70 year-old Klamath Indian believed his termination was wrong; that the First Amendment's guarantee of "Free Exercise of Religion" protected his right to pray the old way. Indeed, lower courts had so held in earlier cases and in this case the Oregon Supreme Court agreed.

But Oregon Attorney General David Fronmeyer disagreed with his own state Supreme Court and appealed to the U.S. Supreme Court. Fronmeyer was busy running for Governor at the time as a Republican and relished the considerable publicity in the press.

The case record showed the particular religion in question, according to anthropologists, had roots in the Americas dating back ten thousand years. No one argued it was not a bona fide and well-established religion. In fact, the record showed that as many as two hundred fifty thousand Native Americans participate in this religion. Not all attend peyote prayer services regularly, but it remains their religious practice in times of need or the giving of thanks. Much the same as other, more "mainstream" religious practices. The record further showed the federal Drug Enforcement Administration had a long working relationship with the NAC through which they, along with Texas, regulated the harvest and distribution of the peyote cactus to the NAC for their religious use. The DEA testified the religious use of peyote by members of the NAC is not part of "America's drug problem."

Over time, the U.S. Supreme Court has evolved a hierarchy of tests which courts apply to determine the outcome of cases where the government's interests conflict with the interests of individuals and groups. For most cases the government only has to prove it had a "rational basis" for its actions and that they treated people equally and fairly. But there has been a higher standard reserved for cases which implicated or challenged the rights of individuals in matters specifically protected by the Bill of Rights – in this case the specifically protected right to "Free Exercise of Religion." The Supreme Court has named the test in such cases the "Compelling State Interest" test. With this test, when litigants demonstrate that a government action interferes with a Constitutional right of a person, the courts scrutinize the government's actions more closely and hold them to the higher standard. The government has to prove a compelling governmental interest is at stake and that no less restrictive means could be devised by which the government could protect its compelling interest. That is a high bar, as it should be in cases involving fundamental rights.

So when this case (here condensed for brevity) came before the highest Court in the land, there was a general perception among court watchers – including the "mainstream" religions - the Court would apply the "Compelling State Interest" test and we would all see how the old religion would fare under its application. The "mainstream" religions did not go out of their way to rally up with the NAC. They assumed the decision, however it came out, would be fact specific and apply only to Indians with their own quirky legal position under our nation's jurisprudence.

But freedom of religion took a dark turn. Five of the Justices signed an opinion written by Antonin Scalia holding that applying the "Compelling State Interest" test to simple, free exercise of religion cases was a "luxury our democracy can no longer afford." From now on, simple freedom of religion cases would only be analyzed by the "Rational Basis" test. That lower standard test asks only if the government had a rational basis when it criminalized peyote use generally, and whether the law was applied in a nondiscriminatory manner. It took Scalia twenty-seven pages to contort logic, history, and morality to reach the conclusion that with the old standards inapplicable, there was no constitutional legal protection for the NAC's use of peyote.

Sandra Day O'Connor wouldn't sign on to such a tortuous rationale, but rather filed a concurrence which said in essence, "Boys, you've gone too far. Let's keep that venerable old Compelling State Interest test and simply rule that the Indians flunk the test." In effect, she didn't have a problem throwing an ancient Indian religion under the bus of modernity, but wanted to keep offering higher standard constitutional protections for the mainstream religions.

Anyway, with her concurrence she joined the other five in making a 6-3 ruling against the NAC. This turned a quarter of a million Native practitioners of an honorable and ongoing religion into felons overnight. To me, Justice O'Connor's Opinion was in some ways even more odious than that of the five she joined. Those of us involved in the case were devastated. This dismissive chilling of bedrock constitutional protections shot right up my spine.

The decision sent shock waves through the entirety of the religious communities and persuasions in America. In the years immediately following such an unprecedented and devastating decision, Congress statutorily tried to restore the integrity of religious freedom both generically and to the NAC in particular. But that's another story. I want to get back to the public toilet in the great north woods.

It was a sunny, summer morning on a northern Wisconsin highway. A couple years had passed since Sandra Day O'Connor retired. My wife and daughter and I were cruising along the highway when they informed me they could use a pit stop. Up ahead waited a roadside Rest Area and we pulled in. The parking lot was empty. As we started to get out of the car, a van pulled in beside us. In it I noticed a male driver with three somewhat elderly women behind him. As my ladies headed for the women's room, one woman got out of the van. It was Sandra Day O'Connor. I recognized her instantly, and confirmed it in my mind when I recalled that her family had a long established lake home in the area. This tall and dignified looking lady followed my two into the restroom. A few minutes later my wife and daughter came out to where I waited in the sun. We stretched a little and talked. Meanwhile, my mind raced with a dilemma one does not often encounter.

Here I stood with this knowledge. My daughter and wife had just shared a private restroom experience with the first woman to ever serve on the Supreme Court of the United States of America. They had peed simultaneously in adjacent stalls. There was no one else around. It was a calm and peaceful moment (except in my mind) rife with opportunity.

What to do? At any moment the woman of incredible national stature would come out that door and walk within six feet of all three of us. On the one hand, what an honor it could be. I could easily catch the moment and introduce my wife and daughter to this woman who made history simply by serving on the Court. We could share handshakes and pleasantries, creating memories for my family.

On the other hand, out from the ladies room door was about to come a U.S. Supreme Court Justice who had sent a grave insult to Native America…to my clients and friends. What should I do?

The time to think was ending. The door opened and the statuesque, gray-haired lady emerged. In the split second left I thought of Scalia and the other Justices she had joined in the result. If it was one of them walking toward us what would I do? Clearly, I would not give any of those men the perceived dignity of recognition. Why bother? If I limit the moment to a simple introduction, he receives additional confirming cachet to his celebrity. If I turn it into more, it becomes an ugly and futile moment, pushing hard on a gate after the horse is gone. Merely a couple egos in a parking lot.

So in a quiet heartbeat I decided to treat Sandra Day O'Connor the same way I'd treat one of her male counterparts. The same scrutiny. As it should be. As her van pulled away we talked about what just happened. There were mixed feelings. My wife and daughter wished they had at least looked more closely.

Time has mellowed me. Made me wiser. If we meet up again, perhaps there will be introductions all around. Perhaps not.

BEYOND ZAROS

Stones as old as the hills they made sit for centuries beside and beneath the road meandering up the hillside through unmarked turns, none of which are wrong.

The walls that make the houses, and from them the villages through which the road winds, are at times close enough to touch from the car window, and are also made of these stones.

The road winds around one last bend delivering you in an instant into Zaros. Now the road becomes a street along which old Cretan men sit at simple marble café tables with their coffee and their prayer beads which flip and clack.

By always staying on the widest street as it offers forks and tempting turns, eventually the street leads around one more bend, putting you in an instant beyond Zaros; once more on the winding country road. Wildflowers splay beside it and olives get crushed upon it.

Here for centuries, warriors and other travelers have coursed beyond the edge of the old maps to where the locals, mostly now gray, have in more recent times made a friendly little lake of the water from the hills. Here the sun, the trees, and the Greeks have together created a quiet, welcome shade for themselves and for travelers to stop at the friendly end of the road beyond Zaros.

THINGS MY MOTHER KNEW

There is probably no point in making nuanced arguments about how Americans, by comparison, turn out a bit more rule-driven, rude, and less helpful to strangers than one finds in the citizenry of most other countries. So I'll just assert it and move on.

Upon return from extended travels one wonders about the cultural advantages to living in the U.S. other than legally turning right on red and flushing some kinds of paper down the toilet with impunity. It is true our coffee cups are bigger. On the other hand, the hotel windows won't open. Also, in the U.S. the average person is less likely to get caught up in paying bribes or baksheesh to get things done. Here in the U.S. such practices remain reserved for big corporations and large government deals.

In "less developed" foreign lands we might encounter more isolated glitches and delays which often cause minor inconveniences. Here we have a low tolerance for such glitches, and have homogenized and sterilized our systems in uniform ways minimizing such problems. Alternatively, system breakdowns that cause significant disruptions are more frequent here. Think of the domino effect in airport delays.

All in all our coffee gets better, and our bread, too. But that doesn't make it much easier to put up with the relative rigidity of our rules. Regulations here in the land of the free get heavier, and we insist on much more stern and unapologetic enforcement than in most other, "less free" places.

An increasing percentage of those freedom-sucking rules were paraded in on a bandwagon of patriotism, supposed to protect us from people from other places. People who a recent President, a particularly untraveled one, declared "hate us for our freedom."

If we acted a bit more neighborly with the rest of the world, maybe that interactivity would render us a bit less selfish and xenophobic, a bit more respectful of others, and less bullish. Then we would make more friends and fewer enemies. This is no great new theory. Or, as my son would say, "It ain't exactly rocket surgery." These are simple and profound applications of universal common sense my mother taught me.

I used to consider my mother's teachings mundane. Now I worry they are unachievable.

HOPE IS PROFOUND, FAITH A MISTAKE

I don't think the true believers in any of the historic religions take life seriously. "Historic" is an academic term in religious studies meaning the long-standing, on-going religions with voluminous written records. The list includes Judaism, Christianity, Islam, Hinduism, Buddhism, and, to a lesser extent, Taoism.

I include Buddhism and Taoism here provisionally because they did not begin as belief systems. Each of them arose as experience based paths to finding wisdom. But in their derivative, contemporary forms they have sunk (in significant measure) into mere systems of belief along with the rest.

All these current watered-down religions demand adherence to unprovable assertions; blind faith. They are patchworks of contradictory beliefs encrusted in translated, secondary, and tertiary texts. All these contemporary religions find themselves riddled with gobbledygook, attempting to come to terms with inherent contradictions and counter-intuitive claims. Add the mandatory, exclusivist prescriptions for something called salvation. Add their self-proclaimed, doctrinaire sense of both superiority and finality. Even within each of these closed faith-based systems lurk claims of superiority between sister sects.

In these belief bubbles, happiness comes from sanctimonious guarantees. Perpetuation comes from manufactured strife and striving.

Great teachings arose in each of these religions, no doubt. I would characterize the great teachings as universal teachings in cultural clothing, though it strikes some as blasphemy. The mythic and archetypal values of the moral and spiritual virtues expressed in these historic traditions have informed and enriched the cultures which have subscribed to them for centuries. But to a point. And that point is a tipping point.

When your beliefs command that your faith in them precludes - even forbids - you from open explorations or more holistic perceptions, then mistakes are made, decisions poorly grounded, dualistic antagonisms fought over (us versus them, me versus nature).

Blind faith puts war on the map, pollution in the water and gold in the Vatican. Blind faith turns a blind eye when human actions cause species to go extinct or weather on earth to change, because this work, this earth, this life, serves as merely a staging ground for the real action in the next world. The pie waits in the sky.

For the above reasons I eschew faith. Why would I choose to believe in faith?

Yet hope remains. Hope we know springs eternal. I may sound pessimistic, fatalistic, like an infidel and blasphemous, growly and snarly. Nonetheless I find resilience in the life force and compassion in the heart. Hope lives, and it lives for us all, of all faiths and none, and of all species. It lives for the water and the weather as well.

Hope adds a vital dimension to living. Absent the tangled knots of faith, hope provides a life affirming propulsion. Hope sends energy to the future.

Epilogue

So They Sued Us

Summary. One day around dinner time in 2013 the phone rang. Someone from a multi-national oil pipeline corporation called Enbridge told me they wanted to run a twenty-four inch pipeline across our farmland capable of transporting three hundred thousand barrels of oil a day. The pipeline would get the oil to a seaport so it could be sold on the world market. Enbridge called the proposed pipeline "The Sandpiper." I told them my wife and I weren't interested. We did not want to participate in their profit-driven project to increase the global warming crisis through the extreme extraction of high carbon fossil fuels.

They kept calling and mailing "sign here" documents by FedEx with prepaid FedEx return envelopes. We kept saying no. They offered more money. Finally we suggested they should just go around our property. They said they were Enbridge and they don't go around anything – they go through it. They offered more money. We said we did not want their money.

So they sued us.

Eminent Enbridge Domain. Enbridge Pipeline Corporation is a multinational corporation based in Canada; the largest oil pipeline company in the world. In the early days of the feeding frenzy created by the discovery of frackable oil in the Bakken oil fields of Western North Dakota, Enbridge moved in. They created a subsidiary called North Dakota Pipeline Corporation, put on nice suits and went to visit with the kind but naïve state government officials. I suppose they said they were worldwide experts in such matters and knew how to help North Dakota plan for the most efficient and expeditious way of capitalizing on the oil boom. The plan included declaring Enbridge a "public utility" and giving Enbridge the power of Eminent Domain. This gives Enbridge the authority to condemn land and take easements for the purpose of constructing its privately owned pipeline. They would get the oil out of North Dakota, through Minnesota, and onto ships in

Duluth/Superior, where it could be sold to the highest bidder on the world market.

It is important to note, unlike a rural water line system or a rural electrification project, the Sandpiper Pipeline would serve no property owners. Indeed, the purpose of the pipeline is to get the oil out of the state (perhaps even the United States) as quickly as possible. The only oil to come out of the pipeline along the proposed route would be from spills and leaks – phenomena in which Enbridge has much experience. More on that later.

North Dakota's Public Service Commission (PSC) had quickly and quietly approved the Sandpiper project, including the proposed route Enbridge had designed. The PSC found it was a safe and suitable route because Enbridge had reviewed it and declared it so. Apparently, it did not occur to the PSC such a process was akin to asking a fox for an objective assessment of a hen house.

Minnesota, to its credit, cast a more critical eye on the proposed project. Coalitions of concerned citizens formed. There were over-lapping groups of farmers, Indian tribes, and environmentalists. Eventually a lawsuit was filed and, in spite of Enbridge's pleas, the Minnesota Court of Appeals said the proposed project would require an Environmental Impact Study under the provisions of Minnesota's Environmental Protection Act.

In North Dakota no coalitions of concerned citizens formed, and North Dakota has no Environmental Protection Act.

Our Land. Both sets of my grandparents farmed in North Dakota. One of them in Grand Forks County wherein lies the land we now own and Enbridge sought to condemn. My father purchased this particular parcel (one hundred sixty acres) in 1980 and it has remained in our family ever since. When my parents died my brother and I divided the farm land they owned between our two families to make it easy for us to pass it on to our respective heirs. That's how my wife and I came to own this quarter section parcel and the one adjacent to it.

Upon inheriting the land we told our children we considered it part of our family legacy. We told them we would continue to rent out the tillable acres to local family farmers and keep the rest in the Conservation Reserve Program, same as my parents did.

When Enbridge contacted us we told them this story. And we told them quite a bit more. We told them about our personal values concerning the environment, the future, our investments, and our sense of responsibility. We told them that from the time we first began to invest money in the market, we focused on socially responsible investments and have specifically excluded investing in, among other things, fossil fuels. We have instead tried to invest in the technology of sustainable energy.

We told Enbridge and their attorneys we drive cars and, yes, we've enjoyed the boons that oil has provided... but it's time for change. As a society we are scraping the bottom of the barrel with the desperation of extreme extraction only to prolong the status quo and the rusty, familiar, technological infrastructure the oil companies own. Our society tolerates this in spite of the toxins and earthquakes of fracking, the flaring off of natural gas, and in spite of the incontrovertible, science-based evidence, in spite of the ill effects on the climate and the natural world - upon which all living things rely. We told Enbridge we see the status quo as short-sighted, shameful, and lazy thinking.

When life presents you with an opportunity, we said to Enbridge, you should take a stand for what you believe in – in this case the future health, balance, and well-being of the world and all things in it. We felt compelled by dignity to rise up to our opportunity.

We told Enbridge we brought our children up this way and our children support our principles. We told Enbridge if we failed to take such a stand, we would be hypocrites, and who wants to be hypocrites in the eyes of their children?

Enbridge offered us more money.

The Supreme Court and Eminent Domain. "Eminent Domain" is the power of a governmental entity to take private real estate for a public use, with or without the permission of the owner. The concept goes back at least as far as biblical times. It appears in the Fifth Amendment of the U.S. Constitution which states, "...nor shall private property be taken for public use, without just compensation."

As the language indicates, the taking of private property has traditionally been limited to necessities of public purpose, such as building a community flood dike or a rural water line to serve residents along its course. The courts have heard many legal battles over what constitutes a "public use" and what "just compensation" might mean.

The scope of what a "public use" means in this context took a dramatically expansive turn in 2005 in Kelo v. New London, a U.S. Supreme Court case. The case involved private homes in a neighborhood area of New London, Connecticut. Pfizer Pharmaceutical Corp. approached the City and said they wanted to build a corporate headquarters along the river where a neighborhood then stood. Their plan included a large parking lot and a park. Pfizer promised jobs and tax revenue. The City gave the New London Development Corporation the power to condemn the land for Pfizer. Many of the homeowners got understandably angry. Some of the homes had been in the same family for over a hundred years. Some residents, now elderly, were born in their homes and never lived anywhere else. They got together and filed a lawsuit to protect their rights to their private property. The case made it to the U.S. Supreme Court which ruled 5-4 that this particular taking of private property for a corporation's purposes did constitute a "public use." This interpretation of the "Takings Clause" of the Fifth Amendment went beyond any previous interpretation of this constitutional provision.

After the city purchased and either moved or destroyed the homes, Pfizer merged with another corporation and decided to change its plans and move elsewhere. The project displaced all the residents, the City lost $78 million, and the parcel of land sits vacant as of 2014, except for the part used as a dump after a hurricane in 2011.

Curiously, although the four most conservative Justices on the Court cast dissenting votes against this expansive interpretation of "public use," my wife and I have found very little support for our position among our Republican friends.

In the aftermath of the Kelo decision, many states enacted laws to insure this broad interpretation of eminent domain would not enable the corporate taking of private property. North Dakota was one of those states and, in fact, by a public referendum of 67%, the public amended their state Constitution to prohibit the taking of private property unless it is necessary for "a common carrier or utility business." In a pathetic paradox, the North Dakota Public Service Commission and our trial court contorted their way around their own Constitution by declaring an oil pipeline is a common carrier, like a railroad, and therefore exempt from North Dakota's new constitutional limitation. The crazy theory goes like this: just like any citizen can put themselves or their stuff on a train, so any citizen can put their oil in the pipeline. Never mind that 90% of the capacity of the proposed pipeline was already contracted for by Big Oil, and the remaining 10% tied up with restrictions effectively prohibiting all but Big Oil from buying space in the line. We thought a jury of North Dakotans ought to hear about this and determine whether it complies with the constitutional amendment they voted for.

Jury Trial. Because our parents raised us to stand up for what we believe in, and because we raised our kids that way, we had to fight. It is expensive, but it isn't hard to do. Change comes from circumstances and pressures and tipping points. While it was unlikely our case would serve as a tipping point, it clearly provided a circumstance for applying pressure in a direction away from fossil fuels and more carbon in the atmosphere and toward a cleaner, sustainable energy future. Therefore we could contribute to the collective will to try to repair the damage of the carbon we put into the atmosphere, and the increasingly irreversible effects on climate and weather around the world.

Human civilization may find the will and the way to undo the damage and retrieve a sustainable healthy natural world like the one we inherited, or it may not. The great anthropologist Margaret Mead said, "Never doubt that a small group of thoughtful, committed citizens can change the world; indeed, it's the only thing that ever has." We do what we can.

Under North Dakota law we had a right to a trial by jury, and we attempted to use that right. We didn't sue the multinational pipeline corporation. They sued us. Because, however, they first got the North Dakota Public Service Commission to declare them a "common carrier," they were in the catbird seat as they bullied their way across the state and out into the world of corporate profit. We wanted to ask a jury of North Dakotans if that was an unconstitutional delegation of the power of government to a private interest for a private purpose. Should Enbridge, a foreign corporation, be able to trump our use and enjoyment of our family property under these circumstances?

We also wanted to ask a jury of North Dakotans to think about their own contribution to the increase of carbon in the atmosphere and their own responsibility to the future generations of people, all other living things, and the sustainable natural systems upon which it all relies. Enbridge took the position that our perspective was irrelevant to this case. Enbridge figured climatic implications are none of our business, and none of the Court's business. We attempted to ask, "Well, whose business is it?" Enbridge tried their damnedest to kick that can down the road by subverting our chance for our day in court.

Although Enbridge fought to exclude "big picture" considerations from the case – a case they initiated – for us it felt like the perfect time, forum, and set of circumstances. If not us, who? If not now, when?

Unfortunately, the jury trial didn't happen. Prior to trial, Enbridge filed a Motion for Summary Judgment. Essentially it said, "Your Honor we are so clearly in the right under the law that you ought to rule in our favor now and not waste the time of the Court or the jury with a trial." We filed a brief in response essentially saying, "Wait a minute. Enbridge sued us! Surely we are entitled to our day in Court to articulate why we don't agree with being forced to participate in their plans."

The Judge ruled in favor of Enbridge, thus denying us our day in court.

These bastards play hardball. They figured we would fold. But we had a strong legal team who believed in our case. We felt we held the high ground, and would wind up on the right side of history. Motivated by the factors discussed below, we quickly determined to file an appeal with the North Dakota Supreme Court.

Climate. According to the 2010 book *Merchants of Doubt* by Naomi Oreskes and Erik M. Conway, the same strategies, and some of the same people, used by the tobacco industry to throw doubt and confusion into the connection between tobacco and health, are now employed by the oil industry and others to muddy the waters on the global warming/climate change issues. The point is simply to keep a controversy and a riddle of doubt alive in order to preserve the status quo (read power and profits). This practice is simultaneously reprehensible and financially successful.

The highly respected journalist Naomi Klein has done a remarkable job of investigating the facts and issues surrounding climate change and has published her findings in a 2014 book called *This Changes Everything*. The facts and figures cited below come mostly from her work unless otherwise indicated. Thank you, Ms. Klein, for your courage, care, and diligence.

Governments and scientists began warning us about the need for radical reductions in greenhouse gas emissions in the 1980's. Since then, while the merchants of doubt sowed their shady seeds, real work was coming together in the scientific community. Let's start with this straight forward assessment:

> *"Climate scientists agree: climate change is happening here and now. Based on well-established evidence, about 97 percent of climate scientists have concluded that human-caused climate change is happening. This agreement is documented not just by a single study, but by a converging stream of evidence over the past two decades from surveys of scientists, content analyses of peer-reviewed studies, and public statements issued by virtually every membership organization of experts in this field."*

- Report by the American Association for the Advancement of Science, 2014

Meanwhile in 2013 in the U.S. alone, the oil and gas industry spent $400,000 per day lobbying Congress and government officials – and that does not include campaign donations during election cycles (Klein, at 149). According to the Stern Review on the Economics of Climate Change, fossil fuel companies receive $775 billion to $1 trillion in annual global subsidies. Yet they pay nothing for the privilege of treating our shared atmosphere as a free waste dump (Ibid. at 70).

Upton Sinclair once said, "It is difficult to get a man to understand something, when his salary depends upon his not understanding it" (Ibid. at 46). It is fair to say that many on the hardcore right feel compelled to deny the existence, or at least the significance, of climate change because accepting the realities upends their political philosophies premised on unregulated, market driven societies. All true. It's doubtful the captains of industry and their supporters truly disbelieve the evidence of dangerous changes in the climate. Rather, I think they fear the solutions. But it is clear that minimally regulated capitalism is not going to voluntarily get us out of this crisis, for it serves as the very force driving us over the brink. However, the right wingers had better wake up and smell the coffee because we need the old virtues of conservative ideology to resolve this crisis. We need to conserve.

A Bum's Rush. Speculation abounds that the various oil interests insidiously engage in jamming the rail lines in order to exacerbate the need for a pipeline. They have created a situation where Amtrak passenger trains running between Chicago and the West Coast find themselves sitting on the sidings in places like Fargo for many hours while oil trains and fracking sand trains tie up the rail lines. Similarly, the grain trains the farmers rely on to get their harvest to market get sidelined as well, creating a crisis in both storage and economics.

Why does this happen? This messy business directly affects interstate commerce and should trigger reasonable regulation and accommodation. Why does privately owned, nonperishable oil destined for the world market receive unquestioned priority over the movement of our people and our food?

A related set of questions cry for reply regarding the flaring off of natural gas. We get the old bum's rush from the extreme extractors. The oil industry controls the conversation and thereby the big picture. We are hornswoggled into taking for granted that this oil must be sought and sucked out and sold as soon as humanly possible, and damn the torpedoes. The torpedoes include, for instance, the rail crisis and the flaring off of obscene amounts of natural gas.

Neither the regulatory agencies nor the general public effectively challenges these anti-social practices. In fact, let's call them uncivilized practices. Why should we allow the horrendous waste of natural gas that does nothing good, but instead throws massive amounts of carbon and other toxic pollutants into the atmosphere? In the Bakken oil fields this obscenity of waste would heat a million homes.

The oil industry tells us they have neither the practical technology nor the patience to capture the massive amounts of natural gas and pollutants spewing fire into the sky. My father taught me if I can't behave responsibly on the field, I shouldn't be in the game.

Fracking. Among the most dangerous practices of the fossil fuel industry in their desperate use of extreme extraction techniques to maintain their status quo are the initially invisible dangers of fracking.

A 2011 study by leading scientists at Cornell University showed the frightening contributions of fracking to the climate change crisis (Ibid. at 143-4). The study found methane emissions linked to fracked natural gas are thirty percent higher than the emissions linked to conventional gas. Such dangerous discharges occur because the fracking process is notoriously messy and leaky at every stage of production, storage, and distribution. According to the Intergovernmental Panel on Climate Change, what makes fracking so exponentially terrible is that methane as a greenhouse gas is thirty-four times more effective at trapping heat in the atmosphere than carbon dioxide.

> "Furthermore, Cornell biochemist Robert Howarth, the lead author of the study, points out that methane is an even more efficient trapper of heat in the first ten to fifteen years after it is released – indeed it carries a warming potential that is eighty-six times greater than that of carbon dioxide. And given that we have reached "decade zero," that matters a great deal.
>
> "It is in this shorter time frame that we risk locking ourselves into very rapid warming," Howarth explains, especially because huge liquid natural gas export terminals currently planned or being built in Australia, Canada and the United States are not being constructed to function for only the next decade, but for closer to the next half century. So, to put it bluntly, in the key period when we need to be looking for ways to cut our emissions rapidly, the global gas boom is in the process of constructing a network of ultra-powerful atmospheric ovens." (Ibid. at 144-5.)

Leaks and Spills.

In 2010 a ruptured Enbridge oil pipeline caused the largest onshore oil spill in U.S. history in and around a tributary of the Kalamazoo River in Michigan. Over a million gallons of oil spilled out contaminating more than 30 miles of waterways, wetlands, and untold numbers of birds and land animals.

> "...it seemed that Enbridge had put profits before public safety, while regulators slept at the switch. For instance, it turned out that Enbridge had known as early as 2005 that the section of pipeline that failed was corroding, and by 2009 the company had identified 329 other defects in the line stretching through southern Michigan that were serious enough to require

*immediate repair under federal rules. The $40 billion company
was granted an extension, and applied for a second one just ten
days before the rupture – the same day an Enbridge VP told
Congress that the company could mount an 'almost instan-
taneous' response to a leak. In fact, it took them seventeen
hours to close the valve on the leaking pipeline. Three years
after the initial disaster, about 180,000 gallons of oil were still
sitting on the bottom of the Kalamazoo."* (Klein at 331.)

Using data from Enbridge's own reports, the Polaris Institute
calculated that 804 spills occurred on Enbridge pipelines between
1999 and 2010. These spills released approximately 161,475 barrels
of crude oil into the environment. (Wikipedia.)

Where Are We? Toxic emissions into the atmosphere rose by
fifty-seven percent since the signing of the U.N. climate convention
in 1992 (Ibid. at 200). This alone provides proof enough the polite,
vague, and voluntary solutions which don't limit free-market capitalism are abject failures. Carbon released into the atmosphere sticks
around for hundreds of years trapping heat (Ibid. at 21). We cannot
stop global warming before it starts. Too late for that. According to
the International Energy Agency, we had until 2017 to take actions
limiting the rise of global temperatures to only 2 more degrees
Celsius (Ibid. at 23). Given our collective inertia and political
ineptitude, our capacity to stop global warming at 2 degrees Celsius
appears most unlikely. I certainly wouldn't bet on it.

Our culture is myopically bogged down in a political and
economic system that has things backwards. It behaves as though
there is no end to what is actually quite finite, such as, clean water,
fossil fuels, and the atmospheric space to absorb their emissions.
Yet our socioeconomic system persists to set strict limits on what
is actually man-made and flexible; the laws, policies, and financial
resources that are adjustable to create a sustainable world.

*"We know that if we continue on our current path of allowing
emissions to rise year after year, climate change will change
everything about our world. Major cities will very likely drown,
ancient cultures will be swallowed up by the seas, and there
is a very high chance that our children will spend a great deal
of their lives fleeing and recovering from vicious storms and
extreme droughts. And we don't have to do anything to bring*

about this future. All we have to do is nothing. Just continue to do what we are doing now, whether it's counting on a techno-fix or tending to our gardens or telling ourselves we're unfortunately too busy to deal with it." (Ibid. at 4.)

That telling quotation from Ms. Klein describes very well why we were eager to insist on the relevancy of climate change to our defense of the Enbridge lawsuit against us.

Meanwhile, Back in Court. When the trial judge granted Enbridge's Motion for Summary Judgment it meant we were denied a trial on the merits. No jury would be asked to consider either climate change or eminent domain. The judge ruled the only thing left to decide was how much money Enbridge should pay us.

In rough numbers, Enbridge had initially offered us twelve thousand dollars. Then they said they'd double it as an early signing bonus. Later, they raised their offer to thirty-five thousand, then thirty-eight. Their last offer was fifty-one thousand, which they then reduced to twenty-five thousand just before suing us. All of these offers were in writing.

The judge said we could still have our four-day jury trial, but it would be about only money. Enbridge filed another motion with the Court, this one claiming none of their earlier offers to us should be admissible in Court because every single one of them had been made in anticipation of litigation and, therefore, technically were negotiation offers and therefore inadmissible.

The judge agreed with Enbridge. During the buildup of the case Enbridge had hired a rural land appraiser who had valued the actual damage to our land that the pipeline would cause at two thousand dollars. We had hired an Agricultural Economist from North Dakota State University who had calculated the actual damage at twelve thousand.

On the morning of the beginning of the trial, with the potential jurors still in their chambers, the judge said the whole scope of the trial was going to be about whether Enbridge should pay us two thousand or twelve thousand or something in between. The case would be limited to actual damages to our land, and not to the value of the easement to Enbridge.

The Enbridge lawyers smiled and readily agreed to pay us the twelve thousand. There was nothing left to fight about. The case was over.

The Appeal. While the judge's Final Order was mostly a victory for Enbridge, the court did impose a couple of limitations on what Enbridge could take from us.

The Easement document presented to each of the eight hundred landowners along the proposed Sandpiper route in North Dakota reeked of lopsided overreach. I still find it hard to believe that each and every one of those landowners, except my wife and me, took Enbridge's bag of silver under those terms.

The terms of the judgment provided Enbridge gets the easement for ninety-nine years. They don't have to do anything with it. They can put whatever they want in it, including additional pipelines. They can sell the easement to any other entity from anywhere in the world for any purpose anytime in those ninety-nine years. As for liability, Enbridge acknowledges responsibility only for damages that occur during their installation of a pipeline. Some of these features are not stated specifically in the document, but the frightening fact is that they are not excluded.

Individuals are free to sign such agreements in exchange for a one-time payment of cash. But in her Final Order the trial judge agreed with us such brinkmanship was excessive overreach when taking someone's property against their will by condemnation. The judge ruled Enbridge had five years to install the pipeline on our land. Use it or lose it. And she ruled the only thing that could be transported in the pipeline across our property was oil, as defined by North Dakota law. This meant, for instance, it could not be used to transport Alberta tar sands, which many believe to be part of Enbridge's agenda for the Sandpiper line.

With the well-reasoned concurrence of our attorney, we quickly decided to appeal. North Dakota has no intermediate court of appeals, so all appeals of trial court decisions are filed with the North Dakota Supreme Court. The high Court gave us a briefing schedule and both sides filed their briefs.

Next came the wait for oral arguments before the Supreme Court in Bismarck which were set for September 21, 2016.

The Stars Align. Meanwhile, 2016 brought seismic changes to the pipeline project. Minnesota came to their senses and a court judgment ordered an environmental impact study of the proposed

route; there was a black hole in North Dakota (our half mile section); the price of oil dropped dramatically; we heard Enbridge's investors were getting cold feet.

Enbridge figured they had to do something. So they announced to their shareholders they were "delaying" the Sandpiper for a couple years and casting their lot with the already partially built Dakota Access Pipeline (DAPL). They bought a little less than fifty percent of DAPL, with a little over fifty percent owned by Energy Transfer Partners. The DAPL route ran from the same Bakken Oil Fields in western North Dakota south to South Dakota and then east to Illinois. With the volume of this giant DAPL pipe being well over four-hundred thousand barrels of oil per day, the percentage Enbridge purchased gave the corporation an amount of volume approaching what it anticipated in the Sandpiper.

While the DAPL project ran headfirst into a chaotic mess of controversy in the summer of 2016, the clock was still ticking toward our oral arguments. Thus began a series of four almost theatrical phone calls. I paraphrase them below.

The first call came a few weeks before the scheduled oral argument. An Enbridge lawyer by the name of Scott called our lawyer Derrick Braaten. Scott wanted to be sure we saw the news that Enbridge had delayed Sandpiper for the time being. He thought perhaps, since the pipeline project was now inactive, we might want to dismiss our appeal, save some time and money and avoid the risk of losing even worse than at trial.

Derrick called me to convey the message. I said they must've been checking to see if I'd been gnawing on old lead paint since last we spoke. We both agreed the fact Enbridge's lawyer called meant they were worried. From the very beginning we'd told our friends we were going to fight this to the bitter end...but they shouldn't bet on us. I was not confident in the North Dakota Supreme Court. But we figured since Enbridge had set aside the Sandpiper and bought into DAPL, it might diminish their argument that they needed to condemn our land for a 'particular public purpose'. We had very few tools in our strategy kit, but we had principled commitment, guts...and maybe a little sense of humor.

I told Derrick to call them back and tell them he couldn't reason with me. Say I was giddy with the prospects of going to court and wholly unreasonable, like a rabid dog! Then pause a few seconds and say, "And his wife is worse." Derrick laughed and said this was going to be fun.

Derrick conveyed the message and Scott downplayed the significance of his original call, saying it was just a casual inquiry and he hadn't discussed it with his client.

The second call came a few days later. Scott was wondering if maybe we'd had time to think and were willing to discuss dismissal. He didn't have anything to offer us.

Derrick called me and I asked him to call Scott back and tell him I'm livid Enbridge put me through this for three and a half years. Tell him, "Botsford says you fucked up his chi." Derrick laughed even louder this time and said he'd be happy to pass on the message.

The third call from Enbridge came a few days later with oral arguments ten days away. Enbridge wanted to know what we wanted. I asked Derrick to remind Scott I was a long-time friend of Winona LaDuke, a true leader in the larger fight against Enbridge, environmental degradation, and for a healthy, sustainable future. Winona is well known to Enbridge. Tell him I just talked to her and she's down at the Standing Rock Water Protectors camp a little south of Bismarck with a bunch of Indians, horses, and attitudes. Tell Scott we're all looking forward to oral arguments in Bismarck. Then tell him what we want is the following:

Enbridge agrees to give us back the easement the trial court awarded them.

Enbridge files a Stipulation with the Supreme Court saying they'll never seek our land again.

Enbridge agrees to pay our attorney fees.

Derrick conveyed the message and the next morning Enbridge made their fourth call advising Derrick to tell the Botsfords, "We'll give them what they want."

And they did.

The Money. Since we already had hotel reservations in Bismarck, we loaded up the car with quilts and vegetables from Krista's garden and our son's organic farm and headed out on a bit of a victory lap. We picked up our lawyers and their families in Bismarck, drove down together to the Standing Rock camp, and delivered the supplies on September 21st, the day our oral arguments would have occurred. Then we drove back to Bismarck and sat down together to do some money math.

In rough rounded numbers, it goes like this. Under the court rules, Enbridge had to pay our attorneys $82,000. We had raised $10,000 toward our legal defense fund through a GoFundMe website, and an additional $3,000 through direct contributions. That makes $95,000 for our attorneys.

The $12,000 the trial court awarded us for damage Enbridge would've done to our property we had left in escrow with the court, so that went back to Enbridge. Nothing gained, nothing lost, because no damage done.

Next we asked our attorneys what their total bill actually was. Only certain itemizations are collectible attorney fees under the court rules so we assumed the actual bill would be higher. It was. The law firm totaled it up to around $115,000. Oh, how I love good lawyers, especially the ones who are also good people. Our lead attorney, Derrick Braaten, partner in the firm of Baumstark Braaten, spoke for the firm in explaining they believed we had been through enough. We were great clients. The issues were ones they believed in. They appreciated the opportunity to represent us and to make good law. They were likely to attract more clients through the publicity of this case, and would use our case as precedent in the future. All in all, they didn't think we should be out of pocket any more than our own personal expenses, and the firm would absorb the remainder.

Dinner was on Krista and me.

The Poetry of Money. Over the course of the case we had paid our attorneys about $65,000 out of pocket. They sent it back. At my desk, glass of wine in hand, I stared at the check. It occurred to me we get to spend this money twice; once for the lawyers and now for some kind of poetic justice to pay it out again.

So we took a hefty chunk of that money and converted our whole rural Wisconsin homestead to solar energy. We installed a photo-voltaic system large enough to handle all our electric needs, plus sell some back to the grid. If we ever buy an electric car we can charge it ourselves at home… and if Big Oil ever comes calling for my soul again, I can answer with breath born of cleaner air.

. . .